Songs Fro

Healing The

To An inspiring colleague,
who has given me
so much & so happy
to have some-one who has
already been on A
'soul' Journey,
lots of love
Mich - x-x -x

Dedication

For my children, Benjamin, Annig and Jamie, and the unborn souls of their brother and half-sister Lucy.

Songs From The Womb
Healing The Wounded Mother

Benig Mauger

THE COLLINS PRESS

Published by The Collins Press, Carey's Lane, The Huguenot Quarter, Cork 1998

© 1998 Benig Mauger

Prayer Before Birth by Louis MacNiece is reproduced by kind permission of Faber and Faber, from *Collected Poems* by Louis MacNiece

British Library Cataloguing in Publication data.

Printed in Ireland by Sci Print, Shannon

Typesetting by Red Barn Publishing, Skeagh, Skibbereen, Co. Cork

Jacket design by Tony Colley and Upper Case Ltd.

ISBN: 1-898256-54-3

Contents

Acknowledgements   vi

Foreword   viii

Introduction   1

Part One: Birth as Soul Experience

Chapter one: Two Births   9

Chapter two: Wounded Mothers   15

Chapter three: Pregnancy   22

Chapter four: I Am Not Yet Born   50

Chapter five: Giving Birth   59

Chapter six: Being Born   97

Part Two: Healing the Wounds of Birth

Chapter seven: The Lost Feminine   122

Chapter eight: Healing the Wounded Mother   135

Chapter nine: Songs from the Womb   145

Chapter ten: Birth Revisited   164

Chapter eleven: The Gift – Transformation   189

Bibliography   200

Index   203

Acknowledgements

As any writer knows, labouring to bring a book to birth is not easy. I would like to say thank you to the following.

To my clients and all the women and men who have shared with me both the joy and pain of coming into life, and without whom the book would not have been written in its present form. A particular thank you to those who afforded me the privilege to be present at their births, both physical and spiritual. I thank you first and from my heart.

To Charles Wansbrough, Ean Begg, Jean Thomson, David Berk, Susan Windisch and Kathy Westwood, who provided me with encouragement and support in the early days of the pregnancy.

To Jonathan Williams, whose sensitive and perceptive editing and advice with earlier drafts proved invaluable and set me on course.

To Don Roberts for believing in me and in the book when I thought all was lost. To John O'Donoghue, Maire O'Regan and Bob McCormack, who read and reread some or all of the text and offered advice, help and encouragement. Particular thanks to Marie O'Connor for her reading of the book and for writing the Foreword, for her friendship and for bearing witness to the relentless birth pangs of a sometimes harassed writer.

To Elizabeth Peavoy, whose sometimes forceful but always humorous strokes of genius helped me guide the book into shape.

To Maria O'Donovan, my editor, who helped midwife the book, and to Helen Litton for providing the index.

To Tony Colley for his sensitive and beautiful graphic design work, providing the book with its cover, and to Maurice Ward, whose free associations helped me give it a name.

To Gillian Doyle and Evelyn Musgrave, whose friendship and proof-reading were invaluable, and to Marie Mills, who kept my house in order.

To my friends and colleagues, who helped in various ways, especially Paddy McMahon, Mairín Ní Nuallain, Ellen

O'Malley-Dunlop, Valdi McMahon, James Ryan, Edmund Ross, Helen Blair, Nicki O'Leary, Justin Carty, Jim Fitzgibbon and Kathleen McSweeney.

To my colleagues in the Irish Analytical Psychology Association for their acknowledgement and support and with whom I found a psychological and spiritual 'home'. To Mitch Elliot of the Irish Psychological Society, who first invited me to speak on pre-natal and perinatal psychology in Ireland and whose belief in and promotion of my work set me on my present course. To Brian Scott McCarthy for his enduring personal and professional support and encouragement.

And finally to my family, both in spirit and physical form, and most particularly to my daughter Annig and son Jamie, who had to make do with countless take-aways and a frequently 'absent' mother during the gestation and birthing of the book. Special thanks to Jamie, who photocopied the entire manuscript at breakneck speed!

And to my own birthplace and soul home, Connemara, which continues to inspire me.

Foreword

In this arresting and beautifully-written book, Benig Mauger has demolished one of the most pervasive myths of our time, namely, that childbirth is a physical experience to be managed by doctors. She offers us a new reading of birth, based on her experience as a clinical Jungian psychotherapist, set against the background of recent research in pre- and perinatal psychology.

Women, she says, who have had highly medicalised births report feeling dehumanised, humiliated and distressed. I recognise these feelings, these words. They were used by women whose experiences of hospital birth I documented in *Birth Tides: Turning Towards Home Birth* (Pandora 1995). In underlining the relationship between postnatal depression and the experience of a difficult birth, Benig Mauger rightly insists on the existence of a relationship which obstetrics, and indeed, psychiatry, has yet to investigate.

She evokes the spectres of child abuse, drug addiction, and adult violence, and discusses the possibility that these may he linked to the experience of medicalised birth, with its substitution of drugs and technology for individual freedom and autonomy.

Over and over again, Benig Mauger draws our attention to the formative nature of the prenatal and birth experience. Only if we continue to believe that the baby in the womb can hear nothing, sense nothing and above all, feel nothing will it be possible for us to continue to allow obstetrics to dominate women in childbirth. This is a book which makes it impossible to ignore the voice, not only of the mother, but also of her child.

MARIE O'CONNOR
Dublin, 1998.

Introduction

Nature and God-I neither Knew
Yet Both so well knew me
They startled, like Executors
Of My identity.
                    Emily Dickinson

All my life I have been drawn to birth. As a child, when asked by others what I wanted to be when I grew up, my answer was always the same – to find a soul mate and have children. I was born and raised in one of the most rugged and remote parts of Ireland. We lived very close to nature, particularly around the time I was born, so my earliest years were spent out of doors. We lived a fairly isolated existence and my friends were the hills, the rocks and the sea. Cats and dogs were also part of my life and assisting at the birth of numerous kittens was a common occurrence. I was fascinated not only by the ease and efficiency with which our cats gave birth, but also by the implicit order which formed part of the natural birth process. Living so close to the beating heart of nature, I felt imbued with a sense of the divine, of God. I was instinctively filled with respect for the mystery of life. I loved the voices of nature, the wind, the sea and since I usually ran around barefoot, I grew accustomed to the feel and texture of the earth. I felt intimately connected with nature.

Though we attended the local church, my family were not unduly religious. For me, God lived outside, in the mountains and the sky, and I did not usually find him in the church. I found soul in the land around my home. In the trees, on the beach, clambering across the rocks, soul was in the waves of the sea and on the hills that changed colour all the time. Nature had a soul – I could smell it and feel it.

Birth held a numinous energy for me, which means it was charged with the fire of emotion. I instinctively knew that everything connected with birth was sacred. It was many years later, when I was training as a psychotherapist, that I understood why. During this time I came across the work of Swiss psychologist, Carl Gustav Jung, and it is Jung more than anyone who has helped me write this book. Jung saw clearly that the greatest malady of the twentieth century is 'loss of soul'. Modern living alienates us from our natures. Urbanisation and the emergence of social institutions have, Jung contended, served to divorce us from our primordial roots in nature and the life of the spirit. Doctor of the soul, Jung was concerned with healing the rift between nature and man. If we cannot find God in nature and in our own hearts, then life loses much of its meaning. Analysis and psychotherapy is about healing the soul.

The quest to heal my own soul took me into Jungian analysis and eventually into training as a therapist. My work as a prenatal and birth teacher was probably the beginning of this journey. As I began work in the field of childbirth, I discovered the nature of my soul wound. It was a birth wound and it had become naturally activated within me at the birth of my own children. Through the women and men who came to see me, I learnt more about the nature of birth wounds. I discovered the depth and variety of ways in which the birth experience affects us and our relationship to others. My own spiritual quest and my interest in the workings of the human psyche took me into deeper research. In the prenatal and birth experience I found what I was looking for. Studies show that birth and what happens in the womb are of crucial importance to later life. The prenatal and birth experience is formative. What happens in the womb and how we are born is significant in our lives. I discovered that many, many people suffer from birth wounds and that our modern way of birth is frequently to cause.

I think that we are collectively suffering from loss of soul in one way or another, for our modern civilisation with its scientific and technological advances demands a price. Modern medicine, which is based on the division of body from mind, places the emphasis on the physical aspects of health. This means that the psychological dimension is neglected. But if you divorce man from his thoughts and feelings, seeing ill-health as organic in nature, you dismiss soul. And this tears at the very fabric of healing, which is concerned with all aspects of being human, both body and soul. Conceiving of illness merely as a physical thing also strips nature of its spiritual dimension. It rips the heart out of man. Neglect of the soul in society at large and modern medical practice in general, has contributed to a collective disillusionment with orthodox medicine. Seeking a more holistic approach to health, people are turning to alternative medicine, natural healing methods and therapists.

Since modern childbirth is medically managed, over time, there has been a shift away from trusting the natural instinctive process, towards a dependence on technology. Fear and the suspicion of nature has caused birth to become increasingly medicalised. This is causing problems. Most of the problems are at a psychological or soul level. Women and babies are emerging from the experience with tremendous pain. Though medicalised birthing practice has arguably made birth safer, it is at a price. Childbirth, I believe, suffers a particularly intimate and deep wound to the soul and it is women and their babies who pay that price. Ultimately though, we all pay the price.

The seeds of this book were planted a long time ago in a maternity hospital in Dublin and even further back, in the emergency unit of a hospital in a remote corner of rural Ireland. The first refers to the birth of my eldest child and the second to my own birth in extremely difficult circumstances. In the second case, the people in attendance then, at the emergency operation of a foreign woman bleeding profusely, did not expect the tiny premature baby to live. That she did live and has been urged to write this book is perhaps a tribute to the forces of life which were stronger than those of death in the soul of the child at that time. The experience of giving birth to my own child in a manner which I found distressing and painful owing to medical intervention, was, I think, the beginning of a need in me to examine the whole area of birth and childbirth practice in general. The way in which I was born has, I believe, had an enormous impact on the way I live and have lived my life, as I believe it has with everyone.

Although this book is a personal statement based on many years of experience as a psychotherapist, mother and birth teacher, I owe a great debt to my clients and to the many women and their families who have shared with me both the pains and the joys of pregnancy and birth and without whom this book would not have been written. Having had the privilege to be part of many births, I have learnt so much about the joys and the pains of the struggle to come into life. Mostly I have learnt to have a deep regard for the instinctive and natural childbirth wisdom inherent in all women and for the courage that, as human beings, we show in the face of tremendous and sometimes painful change. I wish to thank all those who have worked with me. Their birth stories have filled my pages, just as I hope the words of this book will act in a small way as a solace to those who carry a birth wound which still cries out to be understood.

To those involved in the medical care of pregnant women and their babies, I find myself wanting to express regret if I seem to be unreservedly harsh in my criticism of their work. It is not easy to be in the medical profession. One is constantly having to balance the high expectations of modern health care with the need to respect the human soul. This is especially so with birth, which is an inherently natural life process. Many midwives and doctors I encountered in the course of my work were warm and caring in their approach to the care of pregnant women and their babies. Indeed it is through the understanding and compassion of those involved in this work that many positive changes in birth practice have taken place.

Introduction

However, from my own experience and that of those I have worked with, I believe that there is room for considerable improvement in the way childbirth is managed. Every day there are mothers and babies emerging from birth rooms, distressed and traumatised. Babies are born with violence and mothers are being violated. Strong words, but then the birth experience is a powerful event and what happens then is of the utmost import. At a time when social violence, drug and alcohol abuse, mental unrest and emotional disturbance have become a serious problem, psychological eyes are beginning to turn to the birth room. Studies are beginning to emerge which link violence and drug abuse in later life, to drugs in labour and violent delivery procedures. Some psychologists believe that the primal roots of violence are being sown every day in the birth rooms of the world.

Obviously this is serious. It is only relatively recently that the time in the womb counted at all. This time was once considered unimportant, since unborn babies were not conscious, and psychic and emotional life began after birth. Now we know better. We must learn from the work of pre and perinatal psychologists and others involved in this area of work. We must be prepared to listen to the voices of women and those who tell us what giving birth and being born is like.

Authors are often asked what the purpose of a particular work is. I can say what it is not. This is not a manual on giving birth. It is not a 'how to' book. Nor is it a medical treatise. As the title suggests, this book is about soul wounds. More specifically, it is about identifying and healing birth wounds. Witness to sometimes tremendous pain, my purpose is to highlight the importance of the birth experience from a psychological and spiritual angle, and to suggest that we may need to question some aspects of modern birth. In the latter I am not alone. Others, aware of the importance of birth, have written excellent manuals which offer practical help and guidance on how to achieve a fulfilling birth experience.

The book is divided into two parts. The first deals with the experience of pregnancy, giving birth and being born from a psychological perspective, and is laced with many real life birth stories. The later chapters under the general title of 'healing the wounds of birth' takes the reader into the therapy room. I have included clinical material of my own which illustrates the reflection of prenatal and birth experience on future life. Working with the wounds of birth may take many forms. *Songs from the Womb* looks at how prenatal and birth imprints are reflected in therapy, through dreams and the relationship between the therapist and her client. 'Birth revisited' is a chapter on birth regression therapy.

The final chapter emphasises the transformative and healing power of birth and suggests that our wounds can be vehicles for growth, if we are prepared to take up the challenges they offer us. The book recognises that many of us are born with difficulty and that nature being as it is, medicalised and surgical births are a part of our lives. When these become necessary, they must be dealt with in as humane and compassionate a way as possible, so that soul is respected. And finally, since awareness of the importance of birth and prenatal life is inherent to this book, I have suggested a more holistic approach to pregnancy and birth care. This is based on an acknowledgement of the spiritual and psychological dimensions of the birth process alongside the physical.

I hope this book will contribute in its own way to the deepening of awareness which is needed to make changes in the way birth happens. In a time of great change, when many are questioning the validity of modern value systems and searching for truer, more genuine ways to live, enhancing birthing conditions is vital. Reconnection with the natural wisdom of childbirth becomes imperative, if improvement is to take place in the way our children are being born. This book aims to help that process by highlighting the importance of the birth experience and by emphasising the spiritual nature of birth.

Part One

Birth as
Soul Experience

Chapter One

Two Births

It was a drizzly night and Dave cursed as the car skidded slightly on the wet road. He swerved abruptly to avoid the bollard and Maria was flung to the left and groaned.

'For God's sake Dave, mind the-' her expletive was drowned by yet another bout of heavy breathing, as a new contraction gathered force and spread over her like a crashing wave.

It was three in the morning and Maria's waters had broken at home, one hour ago. Since then contractions had come every three minutes and they were getting stronger. It was their first child, and the air was thick with that special blend of excitement, anticipation and anxiety. Though they had both attended antenatal classes and had some idea of what to expect, they had not expected it to happen so fast.

Only five more minutes and they should be there. Dave began to sweat and wished he'd had time to pack the drinks they had bought. What if they couldn't find a parking place? His driving became more erratic and as Maria was again jolted forwards, she wished she'd remembered to get into the back of the car, as their antenatal teacher had suggested. At least she could have leaned forwards to help the pain. And Oh God she hadn't been expecting it to come so fast!

At last, the hospital, and yes, there was plenty of space to park the car. One of the advantages of going into labour in the middle of the night, thought Dave. He was about to say so, but decided against it as Maria leant forwards again, puffing loudly. 'That was a strong one' she said, when she was finally able to talk. She heaved herself out of the car and strode purposefully ahead, hoping she would get safely inside the labour ward before another contraction came. Dave locked the car and carrying her case, hurried after Maria. Inside they were met by Janice their midwife, who'd rushed out as soon as Dave had phoned her. The Jacksons had chosen a 'Domino' delivery which meant that they would be delivered by a midwife they knew and who had looked after Maria during her pregnancy. This was a hospital with a special maternity unit, where the birthing rooms resembled as far as possible a home-like environment. It was very important to the Jacksons, as they wanted a natural birth with as little intervention as possible.

After the initial examination procedures, Maria was declared to be three centimetres dilated and progressing well. Dave unpacked the things they had brought with them, placing the cassette player and tapes on the table. Maria changed into the white cotton nightshirt she had chosen for the labour and asked for some water. Pausing during contractions, Maria and Dave arranged the room to their satisfaction and then settled down to what was already promising to be an exciting, natural birth in a place they felt safe, with a midwife they trusted.

It is six o'clock and the first streaks of dawn have begun to appear behind the flimsy fabric of the curtains, in a room which by now has become stuffy, the air thick with the sweating sounds of childbirth. Maria, now in strong labour, leans over the beanbag, while Dave massages her back. Janice, having listened to the baby's heartbeat, pronounces that all is well, but her voice is drowned by Maria's sudden howl as a contraction reaches its peak and crashes down, engulfing her in pain.

Maria struggles to emerge from the sea of pain and sweat and tears mingle with the blood of birth. The child inside her squirms and heaves as she too is caught up in the struggle to be born. Her sensitive tiny body suddenly gripped by mighty forces, she is squeezed and pressed, she is powerless to move, she can no longer struggle. The force subsides, and she is released once more into the warm watery womb that has been her home for the last nine months.

Mother and child rest awhile, waiting for the mighty force of birth to start again. Meanwhile, a cool flannel, a gentle massaging hand and a long cool drink of water. In the background the fading sound of a Brahms cello sonata mingle with the gentle twittering of the birds as they begin their day. All is quiet in the labour room. Everyone is respectful of nature's majestic power. Dave removes his shirt and tie, and Janice's hair falls loose from its band. The heat has become unbearable. A window is opened, although Janice explains that it will have to be shut again soon, because with contractions like these, the baby won't be long in coming.

An hour or so later, Maria's cries become all too insistent for Dave, who, panicking, suggests some kind of pain relief. Maria snarls at him and Janice busies herself with the trolley, then goes to calm her down, suggesting a soak in the birthing pool. Maria's answer is to grip the midwife's hands and scream, 'I want to push!'

'You can't possibly be ready yet,' says Janice. But the sudden rush of warm liquid from between Maria's thighs splattering onto the tiled floor says otherwise. The child is once again squeezed in a vice-like grip and as if that wasn't enough, this time feels itself being propelled forwards only to be stopped by something tough and unyielding.

Suddenly the room is filled with activity. Basins are placed in strategic places and the little cot in the corner is prepared. The window is firmly shut and all hell breaks loose as Janice attempts to determine whether Maria is in second stage labour and fully dilated. Unable to stop herself, Maria with her next contraction bears down with Dave supporting her from behind. Soon everyone in the room is pushing with Maria, willing the baby to appear. One more rush, the pain is huge. Maria screams and wonders what the noise is. The baby's body is caught against its mother's. She sweats and heaves one more time and there, emerging at last, the little head. 'Hold it, hold it!' Janice's voice is urgent now. 'Pant, don't push.' Maria tries to hold back the force inside her. She pants and puffs, but her body explodes forwards as her child urges to be born. The baby's head is safely delivered with another push and Maria's triumphant scream. One more and her little girl child emerges now, all warm, wet and shiny. She is immediately put gently onto her mother's body, the cord still pulsating, whilst Dave, overcome with emotion, is asked if he would like to cut the cord. Unable to reply, he hugs his wife. There is a moment's timeless silence as mother, father and daughter take each other in.

Janice finishes what she has to do, keeping routine to the minimum, and very soon leaves the new family together. The bonding has begun and the baby, having gazed up at her mother, now suckles contentedly at the breast.

Later, driving home, Janice sighs as she pulls up before her home. It's the warm contented sigh of a job well done, the sigh of satisfaction knowing something good has happened, something very special that happens nearly every day; a little baby girl was born at eight fifteen this morning.

Meanwhile, back at the hospital, exhausted but jubilant, Dave is still busy putting money into the public telephone, telling everyone 'It's a little girl.'

Maria snuggles down with her new daughter, marvelling at the miracle which has produced her, both of them tired with the work of birth, yet triumphant. The little girl searches out her mother's warm breast and Maria, responding already to the demands of her newborn, holds her tightly and sings a silent lullaby.

That same evening, at around six o'clock, a woman is wheeled into room 504. She's barely conscious and attached to a drip. The label on the door of the room says 'Mrs Lloyd'. There is no one with her, apart from the nurse who wheels her in. Mr Lloyd has already returned home. Although this is the maternity unit, you'd never know it for there is no little cot and there is no baby. Mrs Lloyd is settled in bed, the drip adjusted and a nurse set to watch her every now and then.

In the special care unit two floors up, the duty nurse is being briefed. A new baby has arrived, a tiny little premature girl. There is some concern for the latest inmate, only thirty-two weeks and delivered barely two hours ago by emergency cae-sarean section. The nurse peers into the incubator. That little one doesn't look too good, her colour is bad, she thinks. The little girl was born with severe hypoxia, as her mother had haemorrhaged badly during labour. The nurse adjusts the tubes, moving the tiny body slightly. The baby is semi-comatosed, still suffering from the effects of the anaesthetic.

Some time later, Marjorie, drifting in and out of her anaes-thesia-induced sleep, calls out through a haze of pain 'Where is my baby?' 'It's O.K., it's in the special care unit, we have a little girl' replies Jack, not noticing how he refers to their daughter as 'it'.

It's been a long and harrowing day for Jack, at one point not knowing if he would lose not just the baby, but far worse, his wife. It was the Lloyds first baby and if this was anything to go by, it may well be their last. Jack did not think he could ever go through this again.

It had started this morning when he received an emergency call at work to come home. Marjorie was bleeding and it was bad. The birth not scheduled for another couple of months. He arrived to find the ambulance already parked outside their home and his wife being carried out on a stretcher. Sitting next to Marjorie on the way to the hospital, the ambulance siren flashing, he looked at her pale face and felt anxious. Everything had been going so well with the pregnancy, but if the baby were to be born now it would be so small, it might not make it. And Marjorie was bleeding heavily. He bent to hear her. 'Will the baby be all right, will it?' she whispered. Her anxious eyes pleaded with him. Jack could do nothing. He held her hand. Feeling helpless and confused himself, he urged her to be calm. His chest tightened with fear. She looked ter-rible, but he knew he had to reassure her. Marjorie turned her face to the wall. Semi-shocked already, she was losing a lot of blood and felt herself slipping away, far away, her life force seeping out of her and she couldn't stop it.

Precisely one hour later she was being prepared for theatre.

'We must stop the bleeding. The child is in danger. We must operate at once. Though small, the baby has a better chance of survival outside. Inside the womb it will die. We have to take that chance'.

The doctors were adamant. Any reactions to what she hears are drowned in the haziness of the anaesthetic. Soon she will be in the operating room, her body being cut open and her baby removed. The last thing on her mind as she goes under the anaesthetic is her child. Marjorie prays, please save my baby. She doesn't know whether she herself will live or die, or whether or not her baby will survive. It does not matter. It is the same thing.

Afterwards, Marjorie asks to see the baby but it's not possible; besides she may not live. Jack had seen her briefly before she was taken away to the safety of the special care unit.

'They are doing all they can,' says Jack. 'Now, Marjorie, you must rest.'

Marjorie starts to produce milk next day as her body responds to giving birth. Unable to feed her tiny baby, she is racked with pain and given tranquillisers to lessen her distress, and diuretics to reduce the milk.

Upstairs, the little newborn in incubator number six stirs, as yet again, the nurse moves the tiny body from where it has wedged itself against the wall. The baby opens her eyes. The nurse peers down into intense, tiny dark eyes. She pauses, before moving on to her next task.

Downstairs, Marjorie, her body aching for her child, feels powerless. She cannot be with her baby, she cannot be a mother. And in any case, her little girl might die. Gradually, an overwhelming emptiness overtakes her. A wall begins to descend on her heart. She turns her face to the wall, crying silently.

The little girl gazes at the space around her for a moment before closing her eyes again.

Chapter Two
Wounded Mothers

And then I heard them lift a Box
And creak across my Soul
With those same Boots of Lead.
Emily Dickinson

The postnatal ward was full that night. Not surprising, after the previous day's full moon! As I climbed the stairs and strolled along the hospital corridor, my heart sang as I heard the cries of newborn babies. A newborn baby's cry is special and stirs the heart of even the most hardened of mothers. In the postnatal ward, women who had recently given birth mingled with those who were ready to leave the hospital with their new babies. It was easy to tell those who had only just given birth: they had swollen bellies and the far away look of those emerging from a life-changing experience.

It was easy too for me to find Marjorie. She was at the back of the ward, partially hidden by a screen. Hers was the only bed which had no tiny cot beside it. Instead there were baskets of flowers, a chair, a small bedside table strewn with different medicines, tissues and a few cards. Though I knew her well, I was shocked at how she looked. She lay on her side, facing the wall. She appeared to be asleep. Her pretty young face was lined with

15

exhaustion and still held traces of freshly shed tears. Her strong body, so recently rounded with the bloom of her pregnancy, looked thin and scrawny under the hospital blanket. Her little arm lay outside the bedclothes. My eyes instantly fell on the big purple bruise left by the recently removed drip needle. It made her look even more vulnerable and wounded.

'Marjorie, it's me, how are you?' I gently take her hand in mine. She opens her eyes and when she sees me, they immediately fill with tears. 'They won't give me my baby. They say she's too small to suck, I can't feed her. Will you go and see her? Please!' She urges.

'Have you seen her since the birth?' I ask. Marjorie turns away, a dull expression clouding her face.

'I'm too weak to move, it hurts every time I straighten up.' She sighs. 'I feel so tired, so drained.' She reaches for her pain killers. She just wants to sleep.

The birth of a baby is generally a time of rejoicing, particularly when both the mother and her child appear to be physically healthy. But things may not always be as they appear, for the birth experience might have been harrowing. A difficult birth often results in emotional wounding in both the mother and her baby. These wounds, because they are not visible, are often overlooked. They are overlooked because we have been taught that having a baby is a potentially hazardous physical experience to be managed by medical professionals. If we emerge from the experience, relatively physically intact, with a healthy baby, then we have no cause to complain.

Within this environment, it is very difficult for women to acknowledge even to themselves that they are unhappy about their experience. After all, the mother may be told, 'what do you have to complain about; you have a healthy baby, don't you?' It is for this reason that many women keep their negative feelings about the birth to themselves, believing they have no right to feel this way. Moreover, they are told that they should not have had such expectations; after all, no one can predict what can happen on the day.

By the time I began working as a prenatal teacher, I was well aware of women's disillusionment with the medical management of childbirth. Many people questioned some of the practices which had become prevalent in hospitals at that time. Books such as Suzanne Arms' *Immaculate Deception*, though aimed at American readers, had a powerful influence on me and those who already questioned our modern way of birth. Unhappy with the way I had experienced the birth of my first child and pregnant again, I sought an alternative way to give birth. Reading a lot, I was influenced by the work of Frederick Leboyer, Sheila Kitzinger and others who advocated gentle, natural births. Keen to avoid unnecessary medical intervention, I planned a home birth. It was fortunate that at this time the work of French obstetrician Michel Odent was receiving much media attention, so the idea that women might choose a less medicalised birth was not new. Michel's maternity unit reflected his belief that the birth process was inherently natural and that women should be allowed to labour without interference. Medical interference disturbed labour and often led to problems.

Birth Plans

Some hospitals, aware of the growing desire for less medicalised childbirth and fearful of potential litigation, introduced 'birth plans' in which pregnant women record their preferences for the prospective management of their labour and births. This system was designed to offer more choices to pregnant women. Janet Balaskas' *Active Birth* and *New Life*, which focused on practical advice and guidance, offered women ways of preparing for a natural birth. Despite some of these changes though, the reality is that things are far from easy for those who want a natural childbirth in hospital.

'Birth plans' are but women's attempt to be heard above a system which many feel has appropriated something which belongs to them. And reclaiming the birth experience is often fraught with difficulties, with women facing hostility and alienation during their pregnancies when they are paradoxically more vulnerable and less able to fight for what they feel is important. Already feeling disempowered, they struggle on, torn between asserting themselves and not wanting to alienate those whose job it is to help them at this important time. Labelled as uncooperative and unable to find the support they need in order to give birth the way they feel is right, many women face the prospect of childbirth in a negative, even hostile, atmosphere.

To make matters worse, grieving for the loss of the expected and desired birth experience is seldom acknowledged or allowed a place in the emotional life of the new mother. It is expected that she get on with life and forget about 'what might have been'. This means that the pain of losing something precious, a good birth experience, remains unexpressed, causing further problems.

Sometimes it is difficult for us to accept the idea that we can feel and mourn the loss of such an intangible thing as a hope or an ideal. This is partly because as humans, we are often limited by our physicality, so that imagination and the life of the spirit take second place to what we can perceive through our physical senses. But the desire to have a good birth experience is so basic as to be archetypal, which means it is in our nature. So that when this does not happen, it can have devastating consequences, with both the mother and her baby bearing long lasting, psychological scars.

For many years I have worked with women who have experienced some form of post-natal depression. Through my own experience of giving birth, I had come to realise that depressive feelings appear to be almost inevitable, particularly following difficult births, such as those which involve drugs, forceps, or other forms of medical or technical intervention. In our modern obstetric practice, the inevitable focus is on making sure that a healthy baby is delivered of a healthy mother, at whatever cost. But there is a danger that being preoccupied with the physical aspects of childbirth one can overlook the emotional; particularly the negative psychological effects of highly medicalised births. I am sure that the sense of disappointment and confusion many women feel after a difficult birth contributes to postnatal depression.

When I began working as a prenatal teacher and therapist, I was aware of a strong sense of wanting to help women give birth in a manner in which they felt fulfilled. I knew that it was often difficult for women to achieve the kind of birth they wanted and that as a result many experienced the birth of their children as negative, distressing or even traumatic events. From my own experiences of being pregnant and giving birth, I had become conscious not only of the depth and magnitude of the experience, but also of the emotional and physical difficulties which evolved when something 'went wrong' during childbirth. Women who had very medicalised births often reported feeling dehumanised, humiliated and distressed by the experience. I knew that as a result, many of them frequently experienced emotional pain and suffering in giving birth and that this had a profoundly adverse affect on their future lives and that of their babies.

At the same time that I was involved in 'teaching' women to give birth, I discovered the work of Swiss psychologist, Carl Jung and what he had to say made a huge impact on me. In my own analysis, which I had started after the birth of one of my children and later as I was training as a therapist, I began to understand how important the experience of giving birth was for most women and further, how feelings about this experience often infiltrated their lives and their relationships. I saw how the way in which birth happened influenced both the mother's relationship with her baby and the future development of the baby.

From my own experience I knew that there is a need in most women, conscious or unconscious, to experience something sacred when giving birth. From those who came to see me, I knew that most wanted to experience the birth of their child as a fulfilling, joyous and creative act. It seemed that all too often this was denied them, since the psychological and spiritual dimensions of the birth process went largely unacknowledged. I found that I was frequently working with the casualties of a medicalised childbirth system which it seemed, was unaware of the profound psychological and spiritual nature of birth. I saw bruised, depressed and traumatised women, battling to come to terms with an experience which fell far short of what they were expecting.

As I listened to the women in my prenatal classes preparing for the birth they hoped for and saw them return with a birth story very different from what they were expecting, I have been struck by the deep sense of loss they carried, often unconsciously, of the experience itself. Listening to their stories and watching the light fade from their eyes as they recount their experiences, I have been left wondering why this sense of loss remains so very often unrecognised by those who could help. How can someone come to terms with something painful if it is not acknowledged?

These women, like Marjorie, are wounded mothers. They are wounded not because they have given birth to a child, but because the experience in some, or many ways, has hurt them. Often the hurt they experience during the birth of their child touches on other hurts from the past, which formerly lay hidden in their unconscious, or in the darkest corners of their hearts. They are wounded because they have been so hurt that depressed, they may find it hard to feel love for their child or others close to them. Or they may feel love, but it will be tinged with pain. They are wounded because in them, the ability to nurture and to bond with their babies may be damaged, often as a result of their birth experience. They are wounded because instead of experiencing joy in the birth of new life, they feel pain. There may be physical pain, but there is also the deepest pain – that of emotional or soul pain.

I am often asked what I mean when I talk about the wounded mother and soul pain. Since those who ask usually know that I am a Jungian psychotherapist, they sense that the wounds I refer to are emotional wounds, wounds to the heart of a mother, pregnant or having just given birth to a child. What I mean and who indeed is the wounded mother are questions that I hope will be answered by the readers of this book, many of whom will be wounded mothers themselves, or at the very least, children of wounded mothers, as we all are in a larger collective sense.

Our personal wounds, as well as our aspirations are merely part of and reflections of, humanity's suffering. To be born is to take on the pains and joys of living as they evolve in the course of one's earthly existence. And our soul, though individual, is also part of the world's soul and both are found in the many things that make up nature, art and the life of the spirit. In this way the wounded mother is not only the woman who, after having given birth lies alone, crying out against the powers that are preventing her from holding her baby, or the woman who bruised and dazed, gazes at a baby she is too anaesthetised to see or feel; or even the vibrant young woman who is wheeled in, exhausted, to the operating theatre, her young body to be cut open to remove her child. The wounded mother is also the lost voice of Mother Earth, unable to articulate her outrage at the desecration of her forests and rivers and the frozen and immobilised voice of the feminine in our collective consciousness.

In the next three chapters we will look at the *experience* of pregnancy, giving birth and being born. In the stories of the women and their babies, you will hear the individual voices of the wounded mother. Later in the book, we will look at the lost feminine in our culture; a story of alienation from nature and loss of soul.

Chapter Three

Pregnancy

It was a fine June morning, the sun was shining and a light breeze held the promise of warmth. Opening the door to the birth centre, I thought, not for the first time, that it was a nice time of the year to have a baby. Minutes later, women in various stages of pregnancy began arriving. The weekly antenatal class was about to begin.

'I thought I might not be here this morning,' sighed Alicia, now overdue by five days. 'Last night I really thought something might be happening,' she said, plonking herself down heavily on the large cushions that lined the walls.

'How are you feeling? Have you got any contractions?' Patricia asked; she had six weeks to go. This was her first baby and she couldn't·imagine what it might be like to go over your due dates.

'Fine, but I just hope they are not going to induce me,' said Alicia. Turning to me, she asked: 'Is there anything you can do to make it come on?'

'My sister took castor oil and she swears by it,' Carol suggested.

Liz piped in 'Well, I tried that the first time and all I got was a bad case of the runs!'

Alicia wasn't convinced and asked me for some tips on how to induce labour.

Pregnancy

The aim of the class was to prepare for labour and birth through regular yoga-based stretching exercises and relaxation. In addition to techniques such as breathing and relaxation, women received information and counselling on many aspects of childbirth. They learnt a lot from the teacher and from one another. The regular weekly classes meant that women got to know each other and came to trust one another enough to begin to express their innermost thoughts and feelings. As one left to have her baby, often returning to the group later to proudly show off her child and recount her tale of the birth, another arrived in the earliest stages of pregnancy. There was always constant movement. For many, the group provided a safe haven, a place to go and be yourself. Whether it was to complain about the aches and pains of pregnancy, or grumble about the long waits at the antenatal clinic and what the doctor had said, or simply to obtain sympathy and nurturing from the teacher, each individual woman came with her own needs and expectations.

Although the focus of the class ostensibly was to prepare for birth, using body work such as yoga-based stretching and toning to enable the body to comfortably accommodate the growing baby, the emotional needs of the women were also considered. The relaxation period at the end of each class provided busy and often tired and stressed pregnant women, with the opportunity to unwind. Each relaxation period included a simple guided fantasy exercise in which the participants were invited to go on a journey to explore their inner world. This technique which is known as visualisation, is a way to connect with the unborn baby nestling deep under the heart of a pregnant mother. Making a connection by way of visualisation with the child you are carrying can be a very healing and valuable experience, since the growth of a human soul from tiny fetus to full term baby all goes on in darkness, deep inside the body of its mother and can sometimes be forgotten because it is not seen. Pregnant women who prepare for their forthcoming birth experience in this way, feel that they are doing something positive. They are preparing both physically, mentally

23

and emotionally for an experience which for many is the most important in their lives.

Great Expectations

There are as many variations in responses to pregnancy and birth as there are women, but certain characteristics are commonly found amongst the group of women who have decided to attend preparation for childbirth classes. Most will want to experience the birth of their babies as fulfilling and enhancing and will want to bond with their new babies. Many will want to gain skills and techniques which they feel will arm them for the forthcoming 'ordeal', and some will want to learn how to cope with the physical pain of childbirth.

Some thoughts and expectations are unconsciously held during pregnancy. For a vast number of pregnant women, especially if this is not their first baby, there will be expectations relating to the past. In other words, women who have had a bad experience of childbirth will often want to make it right the next time. They will seek to heal a birth wound through having a good experience of childbirth. This means that each new pregnancy will be laced with very definite expectations or wishes. Sometimes this makes it difficult for a pregnant woman to approach her new pregnancy with openness and without setting up ideals, for if we already have an image or fixed idea about something, we are often blinded by it and do not see what we have, or where we are. In our pursuit of a set goal, we may obscure reality, but more seriously, we will not be able to value our experiences. Living up to high expectations is not easy and sometimes in pregnancy, hopes of having a good birth are projected by many women onto birth teachers and onto doctors or midwives, since it is these people who will help women give birth.

'Last time, with the caesarean, I felt cut off from what was happening and it took me ages to even want to hold Debbie, let alone bond with her. I felt I had to get to know a little stranger and that I hadn't actively given birth to her.'

Betty was desperate to give birth naturally this time. She

'wanted to be there'. Painfully, her chances of doing so are medically reduced, due to her previous caesarean. Achieving a natural birth after a caesarean can be an uphill struggle, not so much because the woman will be physiologically unable to give birth, but often because the medical profession need to be convinced. Medically, she will be considered a 'high risk' patient and will therefore have to fight that much harder if she wishes to give birth naturally.

Cascade

Many pregnant women do not want to be induced, preferring instead to go into labour spontaneously, thus avoiding the need for medical intervention which would mean interfering with the natural process of birth. Again, it is very common for women who have had an experience of induced birth to want to avoid it the next time. Being induced usually means a more medically managed labour and birth, as one form of intervention will almost invariably lead to another. If labour is medically induced, this forces unnatural uterine contractions on the woman who, because they are more painful, will often need further medication such as anaesthesia, which then often leads to a forceps delivery because the woman is now too numb to feel the urge to push her child out and so on. And because of the drugs used in labour, the newborn may then need an antidote in the way of another injection and so on and so forth. This occurrence in labour is termed a cascade of intervention by those who work in childbirth and is quite understandably, something to be avoided if at all possible. Women who have experienced this kind of birth often report feeling cheated or disempowered. They feel robbed of the satisfaction of feeling that giving birth was the successful outcome of personal effort.

Wounded Feminine Pride

Childbirth is often intimately associated with self-esteem and some women suffer a deep sense of wounded feminine pride

25

when the birth has not been 'natural', or when medical intervention appeared necessary in order to deliver the baby. Again, this is more likely to happen with women who harbour a deep-seated need to heal old birth wounds. For many women, pregnancy and childbirth presents an opportunity to rewrite the stories of the past. This may not always be a former experience of giving birth, but may go back to unresolved issues in childhood, often the mother's own birth or another family experience.

The class is by now in full swing and we move on to the yoga sitting postures. The women sit crossed-legged in a circle, while I call out the benefits of the tailor position. Betty picks up her cushion and says she needs the support of the wall behind her. Alicia shuts her eyes and sighs as she lets her breathing descend deep into her belly.

'She's preparing; it might be tonight!' Patricia nudges Carol.

'This position hurts my varicose veins,' she adds, looking accusingly at me. I try to suggest variations on the tailor position but tell her that she must rest with her legs up as much as possible. This leads to a small discussion on varicose veins and a couple of the women exchange advice on the best treatment available, given that varicose veins are unlikely to be alleviated during pregnancy.

The room begins to feel too hot and I suggest that we move on to the knee-chest position, which, as well as being a good position for various stages of labour, is also very relaxing. This yoga posture involves sitting back on the heels with knees to chest and back extended forwards on the floor. The women settle into the posture. Silence falls over the room and I intuitively know that each woman has entered a different space. There is a natural, physiological relaxation after bodywork and the women settle down often eagerly awaiting the opportunity to relax.

Prenatal Connection

The guided visualisation exercise enables the women to journey deep inside themselves to connect with their unborn babies. I have come to regard this part of the class as extremely important, if not the most important aspect of preparation for birth. The pregnant woman's connection with her unborn baby is a kind of prenatal bonding which will undoubtedly enhance her future relationship with her child.

After the class, there is always time for tea and a discussion. At this time, the women will very often speak about something which 'came up' for them during the relaxation and visualisation. This happens because when we are in a deeply relaxed state, it is easier to become aware of normally hidden, unconscious aspects of ourselves. The relaxed state allows fantasies or images to emerge naturally from the psyche. These are generally sources of information about inner aspects of the person, which can then be worked through on a conscious level and integrated into, or made part of the personality. This is a process that has formed part of my prenatal classes for many years. Additionally, a pregnant woman may visualise her unborn baby perhaps for the first time and may even be able to communicate directly with him or her.

I was able to share an experience of this nature with one woman who did so. Carol told me that after her baby was born, it was to her great delight that her child emerged from the womb exactly as she had imagined her, with brown hair, blue eyes and a short nose like her mother! So, with the teacups and sachets of herb tea, come the hopes, fears and expectations. They are received, dissected, made sense of and finally digested.

Inside Story

For some women though, looking too deeply inside can stir up thoughts and feelings which may appear threatening and unwanted because they cannot be contained. For example, a pregnant woman may suddenly become aware of thoughts about herself or her baby which are too awful or too painful to hold onto, or she may become aware that there is part of her that does not want to become a mother, or who fears becoming a mother. Becoming aware of thoughts or feelings of this nature can be very disturbing, though ultimately potentially healing, if the woman can work through them on a conscious level. This is particularly true of the woman who may be battling with ambivalent feelings about her pregnancy. She may *consciously* be pleased that she is pregnant and may welcome her unborn baby, but the inside story is different. Her unconscious and her body knows this only too well and sadly, the story is often told in her difficult labour and birth, or similarly in her first months as a mother.

In the birth room, I have been privileged to be the witness to many inside stories. Working with the body uncovers the story in a different way from inside the therapy or consulting room, where it is told in words. Pregnancy and childbirth are transitional phases and a time of physical and emotional change. Each pregnant woman is in a state of becoming. She is not what she was, nor is she yet what she will become and this makes her very suggestible and susceptible to the environment and the influences of others.

The atmosphere at the birth centre is a positive one. The focus is on enabling rather than disabling, on empowering rather than disempowering and on taking responsibility for one's health rather than handing it over to an 'expert.' In making the decision and the commitment to come to regular antenatal sessions, each pregnant woman is taking a vital step in becoming responsible for her health and well-being. Here each woman is encouraged to take care of herself rather than to surrender to the ministrations of medical professionals, as is so often the case in the antenatal clinic or hospital. This emphasis on personal responsibility is important, because having a baby is a natural, instinctive function for all women and not, as we may be led to believe, something you have to learn to do through a course of lessons. Antenatal education in this context is misnamed.

Inner Truth

At the birth centre, each woman is encouraged through various ways, to tap into her own instinctive and inner truth, to go back in time as it were, to connect with aeons of childbearing women before her and harness the ancient wisdom and innate knowledge of childbirth which lie in the deepest layers of her psyche. In Jungian language, each woman is facilitated to connect with the archetypal Nurturing Mother.

Repression of the feminine in modern western society has meant that pregnancy and childbirth are often fraught with difficulties. The mother role is devalued and the experience of childbirth is managed and controlled by a medical system largely alienated from nature. This in itself has created a need for antenatal education or *re-education*, since a general estrangement from natural processes means that when women become pregnant, they often feel that they no longer have the tools necessary to bring them through the experience of childbirth safely and confidently. Working in the way described, which endeavours to harness the innate childbearing wisdom of all women, each woman's self-assurance is enhanced, so that she can approach labour and birth with increased confidence in her own abilities.

By its nature, birth preparation has to be holistic, involving both body and mind. The recognition of the unity of mind and body is inherent to yoga-based preparation for birth. This experiential way of working is in contrast to much of current antenatal education that concentrates on information giving, which involves the mind, to the exclusion of the body.

Touching the Soul

When teaching methods are confined to the rational function, such as in lectures and seminars, then it is the left-brain which is used. Right brain learning involves the use of the body or of the mind in a more creative, experiential way such as movement, fantasy or dreams. Our right brain is more connected with our instinctual, natural, intuitive selves and therefore will serve us better when we are engaged in a primal experience like birth, which demands that part of ourselves. Giving birth is an initiation. It is a soul experience. And initiations, to be effective, need to take place in context; that is, within the framework of and supervised by, the wisdom of the ancients. This means that to honour the experience of childbirth, we need to reconnect with the ancient childbearing wisdom of our ancestors. To harness this wisdom our souls must be touched. This is unlikely to happen when we are reading a book or manual on childbirth, unless of course we are moved. We can reconnect with this knowledge through the use of movement, relaxation and visualisation which will facilitate the emergence of our own psychic images. Working with the images our soul produces will enhance our experience and initiate healing if that is needed. Psychic images will give us information and may awaken us by putting us in touch with aspects of ourselves we need to develop in order to grow psychologically.

Within the 'biomedical' model, out of which modern antenatal education has evolved, the emotional, psychological and spiritual aspect of preparation for birth is frequently absent. This emphasis on learned knowledge, fosters the belief that a pregnant and labouring woman can use her mind to control her body. In this light, pregnant women view labour and birth as ultimately medical events. This makes it difficult for women to believe they have any of the resources necessary to give birth through their own abilities. Labour is seen to be managed by the ministrations of professionals.

In contrast, I have found that women who prepare for birth through a combination of bodywork and other techniques have greater resources to draw on in the birth room, whatever the outcome. Most will be more in tune with their labours and better prepared for the experience. It may be that a woman may want and prepare for a natural birth, but finds that on the day, for whatever reason, she needs the help of medical procedure to deliver her baby. It appears that these women feel more in control of their experience and less disabled by it, even if they have had medical intervention. Whatever the outcome, what counts is not what happens, but ultimately how each woman will feel about the experience.

These ways of preparing for birth strengthen a woman's

natural abilities and self confidence, enabling her to then approach childbirth positively. Physical exercise and more particularly yoga-based stretching, is an integral part of this preparation. Bodywork has the effect of grounding the individual in the experience. Pregnancy is a bodily process, so becoming aware of physical sensations is necessary in order to be fully present in it. At soul level, childbirth is an archetype which manifests both in the psyche and in the fibres of the body. Psychologically and spiritually, to become grounded is to become incarnated, that is to fully take on one's total humanity.

Betty stays behind after the class. She wants to talk to me about the possibility of me being at the birth of her baby. Although coming regularly to the group has helped her feel much more at ease, she fears that she may be prevented from having a normal birth. Her second pregnancy is laced with memories and carries a sadness from the past. Her task is a difficult one and Betty needs extra support. Although she desperately wants to be given a chance to prove herself by giving birth vaginally, the hurtful reality is that it will be difficult for her to do so. Labelled as high risk by the medical profession, she is considered incapable of giving birth herself until proven otherwise and this pushes her into doubting herself and falling back on inner insecurities.

'The doctors at the hospital are making it so difficult for me. I have to fight for everything. I sometimes feel it would be easier to just give in.' Betty says with tears in her eyes. 'I feel so useless, maybe I won't be able to do it, but I think at least I should have a choice. After all, I'd like to be given a chance to have the baby naturally and if it turns out I need a caesarean, then at least I'll have known that it was the right decision.'

I understood Betty very well. She was a warm and gentle woman with large sad eyes. I sensed this sadness had a lot to do with her last birth experience and I hoped that somehow this time, she might manage a natural birth and so heal the pain she still carried. She had large, capable hips and looked every inch a mother and I knew that for her the pain of not having been able to push her baby son out herself, still deeply affected her. Her disappointment and fear that the experience would be repeated hung uneasily around her, along with expectations of getting it right this time.

Later, putting the tea things away, I wonder why it is often so hard for women. Inwardly sympathising with Betty's situation, I note her dates in my diary. Betty and I will need to have several meetings as we work through her unresolved painful feelings of the past. This is essential preparation, so that Betty will be freed to face her new birth experience with ease. To meet her expectations may be difficult if these are too rigidly held. But by releasing the emotions of the past she is likely to be less fearful. Hopes and expectations can become crippling if they are too rigidly held and can prevent us approaching life and new experiences openly.

I will also meet with Betty's husband, because if we are to be birth partners, then working together before the birth date is essential.

Celia's Inner World

'Sometimes I'm afraid of going mad!' Celia said, leaning forward on the couch. This wasn't the first time she had said this. I nodded knowingly and asked her to say more about the dream she had had the previous night. Wild dreams and fantasies that seem crazy in the light of day are far from unusual in pregnancy. Celia had been having regular dreams about the baby. 'It' was sometimes born already, but instead of being little and naked as a newborn is, it was fully grown and dressed, or more alarmingly 'it' was a weird animal or even bacon and sausages! We laughed at the idea, but at night Celia did not laugh as she, like thousands of other pregnant women, was bombarded by her crowded inner world. The dark world of the unconscious becomes more accessible during pregnancy and it sometimes frightened Celia.

Celia was a small dynamic young woman with a bubbly personality. She was seven months pregnant and looked beautiful but somehow frail. Looking at her, one wondered how she managed to contain her baby and everything else that was happening, inside her. She had such a small frame and yet it seemed as though the whole world was around and in her, like an over-stuffed drawer. Though small and neat she was vibrant and alive. Being with her, you felt as though life in all its colours and sounds were present all at once.

'I don't know what I am carrying. I mean, it's all happening inside and sometimes when I feel the baby I imagine it with a whole pile of hands and fingers or something.' Celia sighed, resigned to her fate. She had had a good pregnancy so far though and the darkness of her night fears was in stark contrast to the daylight bloom of her body and her glowing health. She was happy to be pregnant; she had waited a long time for this and, though surprised when it had happened, she revelled in her growing bulk. At the post office the other day she had felt proud when she attracted the glances of a number of people, one of whom remarked, 'It's a boy; you've got that kind of shape, all in the front!' She knew she looked good, with her mane of long golden hair and even her skin, usually a source of anxiety to her, exuded health and freshness.

'If only I wasn't so emotional' she sighed. Celia had told me that she had been reduced to tears by a casual remark at the antenatal clinic. Someone had said that she looked 'too small for dates' and had begun to recount her own sorry tale of tests and admissions to hospital, resulting in the early induction of a small baby who needed special care. Celia had gone home and cried as she looked at herself in her bedroom table mirror; cradling her belly, she had imagined herself first dissected and then the mother of a scrawny, barely alive baby. 'I'm sorry Mrs Jones, there isn't much we can do,' she heard the doctor say. Shaking herself out of her fantasy she phoned her mother.

'What size was I when I was born?' she asked. Celia's mother had reassured her, telling her that she was a normal healthy size at birth. But even so, Celia was anxious about herself.

She looked forward to her weekly therapy session, because no one else seemed to understand how she was feeling. At least she knew she mustn't be going mad, or her therapist would have said so. Anyway, it was all so paradoxical; it wasn't that she was feeling bad, only that she felt vulnerable much of the time and irrational, or that's what Simon, her husband seemed to think. Simon wasn't being supportive and Celia was anxious about how it would be at the birth because if he was to be there, she needed him to be more involved than he had been. Terrified of the pain she imagined she would have to endure in labour and unable to speak to him about her fears, she and Simon had started antenatal classes. But even there, it was hard to say what she really felt.

The previous week at the showing of a film on labour, Celia had felt traumatised by what she'd seen and knew instinctively that Simon and the other couples had felt the same. If only they could have talked about it, discussed it, it might have helped to dispel their fears, but there seemed to be no time. Anyway, she knew by the speed and silence with which everyone (all first timers) had left the room after the film that no one knew what to say. Frozen with fear, Celia had come to her therapy session the next day. She spoke to me and I listened and gradually Celia found that in the telling, her fear dissolved, so that some days later, she felt able to approach her prenatal teacher about the film and to begin to discuss her own prospective labour.

There is nothing unusual about Celia. She is a normal healthy pregnant woman with her own particular brand of emotional and mental influences which will be brought to bear on her experience of pregnancy and childbirth. It is easy, however, to think about pregnancy merely as a physical condition and to forget about the emotional or psychological side of things. And yet, as Celia and countless pregnant women know, the physical changes are but one aspect of carrying a child and the myriad other changes, mental, emotional and psychological, are no less dramatic because they are not apparent.

Pregnancy

When we think of pregnancy we most often think of its physical aspects. Stomachs bulging with the growing baby and
enlarged breasts forcing several visits to maternity shops seeking suitable clothing; signs and symptoms of different stages of
the pregnancy indicating regular visits to the antenatal clinic or
doctor and labour and birth arrangements. When we cast our
minds back to the beginning of all this, we think of conception.
There is a magical ring to the word conception, referring as it
does to the beginnings of a new human being. How does it all
happen we wonder, for though equipped with an understanding of our biological functions, nothing prepares us for the
sense of awe we feel when we first discover that we have conceived and a new life is beginning inside us. Conception con-
jures up images of the frantic race of millions of sperm desperate
to reach their goal, of the Herculean task of the one sperm
which will finally penetrate the egg, of the mystical fusion of
egg and sperm and finally, of the tiny, fertilised ovum embedded in the uterine cavity. And it all goes on before the newly
pregnant woman is even aware that she has conceived.

For the woman it has already started, this journey into
motherhood, for whatever the outcome of this particular conception, the seed has been planted and the potential to become
a mother has been activated. As the tiny embryo begins to take
root, it already starts to influence changes and developments in
the woman, pulling her into the depths of her psyche as it activates her 'inner mother.' Not only will pregnancy bring changes
that will shape her body, it will also influence her emotionally
and mentally and it will change her psychologically.

Pregnancy is an experience which will change a woman
forever. No longer will she be a daughter only. She is already
beginning her transition from daughter to mother. Before conception happened, the psychic idea of it existed deep inside her.
Deep inside her too, live the stories and mythic images of being
a mother that have been handed down to her through the generations of her family. The inner mother is that part of a woman
that lies inside, her psychic space, like her womb space, already
pregnant with the potential to become a mother. The pregnant

woman will not only be influenced by the physicality of her new condition. She will be influenced by her inner mother. The inner mother represents in a woman all that is available in potential to be a mother. And it is the interrelationship of biological, social and psychological factors that will shape a pregnant woman's transition to motherhood.

Let us look at pregnancy more closely, keeping in mind the multiple dimensions of the process as it begins to unfold as soon as conception happens and the newly pregnant woman becomes aware that she has conceived.

Body and Soul

To understand what is going on psychologically, it is necessary to look closely at the physiology of pregnancy, for it is the interrelationship of physical and emotional forces that produce changes in the mother. As soon as conception occurs, enormous physical changes begin to take place in the body of the newly pregnant .woman owing to the effects of specific hormones – progesterone and oestrogen. These hormones are normally present in the non pregnant state, but when pregnancy occurs their presence is amplified. The woman's psychological state is affected by these hormonal changes and these changes interact with other external factors such as the woman's history and relationships. The interaction of bodily processes with psychic and emotional elements will influence her transition to motherhood.

I will first outline the physiology of pregnancy[1] and then the psychological parallels. For the sake of simplicity, I shall call the physiological changes '*body*' and the psychological changes '*soul*'.

Body changes: There is an immediate increased level of progesterone in the woman's body. This hormone's function is to relax the mother and to inhibit the natural contractions of the uterus and the rejection of the fetus. As well as being a muscle relaxant, progesterone softens and loosens ligaments and joints, in order to accommodate the baby. This means that the pregnant woman needs the protection of strong muscles to support her growing weight and her more flexible joints and body structure. The pelvic area in particular is where this is felt, as the pelvis widens and opens in preparation for the birth.

Soul changes: There is a psychological parallel. The relaxation of body boundaries results in a similar relaxation of psychic boundaries. This means that the pregnant woman has access to unconscious processes not generally available to her. Raphael-Leff's detailed psychoanalytic examination of the psychological processes involved in childbirth illustrates this aspect of pregnancy extremely well. Indeed, this 'psychic permeability'[2] explains much of the pregnant woman's psychological state and, in particular, her openness and vulnerability to all sorts of forces both internal and external to herself. This is apparent in a degree of emotional instability and in vivid dreams and fantasies.

Inner Pull

The inner pull of pregnancy will make her dreamy and preoccupied with herself and her growing baby and less and less interested or involved in outside events. She will become aware of inner thoughts, fantasies, feelings and conflicts that she may not have had before. She may have vivid dreams, or flashes of insight that may disturb her, upsetting her previous balance and turning her life upside down. Since this loosening of internal barriers includes access to different states of consciousness, it can appear overwhelming to the woman already battling with perhaps unfamiliar mood swings, intense urges and internal conflicts.

So the physical 'instability' is paralleled by a form of psychological 'instability' if you can call it that. Nothing is the same. Things are changing, something is happening inside her which the pregnant woman cannot control. Many pregnant women find themselves unable to maintain the level of emotional discrimination they have been used to. During pregnancy, it is common to be uncharacteristically prone to irritability and the increased vulnerability that marks pregnancy can lead women to become easily upset. Some women in my groups have been reduced to tears by insensitive, if inadvertent, remarks made by the doctor or midwife at the antenatal clinic. The loosening of psychological boundaries and defences means the emergence of conflicting forces in the inner world of the pregnant woman. On the one hand, the psychic permeability of pregnancy allows her to contact her inner world and to be open to change, to growth and to potential transformation. On the other hand, however, it means a disintegration and dissolving of the old structure; it means change and instability which may threaten many women and cause anxiety, fear and insecurity.

Heightened Emotionality

Body: There is a dramatic increase in the blood volume in the body throughout pregnancy. This is in preparation for nourishing the growing fetus and building up the placenta. There is increased vascularity generally to supply blood to the placenta which will (at 12 weeks) take over the function of nourishing while at the same time removing harmful substances from the growing fetus.

Soul: Having extra blood in the body is symbolic of heightened emotionality. Blood has long been a metaphor for feelings and our language is studded with metaphorical phrases such as 'her blood is up', 'it made my blood boil' and so on. Increased cardiac output means that pregnant women have more 'heart' and are more prone to panic attacks and heart palpitations. They are universally closer to their feelings than in their non-pregnant state and many will cry and show their emotions in an uncharacteristic fashion. In this way, becoming and being pregnant sometimes serves to put the normally emotionally detached woman more in touch with her feelings.

Body: The uterus enlarges dramatically and thickens its walls to protect the growing baby. The growth of the uterus starts immediately and continues to increase so that by the end of pregnancy, it is fifteen times its normal weight and almost four times its length. At the same time breast tissue is enlarged to prepare for the task of nourishing the baby once it is born. It is the responsibility of the hormone oestrogen to ensure the mother's capacity to nourish the fetus and the enlarged uterus acts as a container to protect the growing baby. The umbilical cord connects the baby to the placenta and within it are two major blood vessels, one taking oxygen to the baby and the other removing all waste products.

Soul: Just as the uterus enlarges to contain the growing baby, the pregnant woman's capacity to contain feelings and conflicting forces within her are enlarged. As we have seen, this is often very difficult due to the magnitude of internal forces suddenly bombarding her. For the first time since puberty maybe, she is experiencing loss of control. She may have access to thoughts, feelings, urges and fantasies which upset her natural equilibrium. Her body is changing and growing in all sorts of places. There is a live being growing inside her, she is emotionally charged and as if that wasn't enough, at night she is prey to wild dreams and primitive fantasies from her crowded internal world.

Yet, alongside all this is an instinctive desire to nourish things. She may become interested in children and small animals for the first time in her life. She will cry when watching films which involve the mistreatment or cruelty of children, she may become a champion of the vulnerable and the underdog. She may also feel the need to pamper herself. Her visits to her mother or a mother surrogate will increase in an unconscious effort to obtain the mothering she needs. She will almost certainly project this need onto the health professionals responsible for her care, who will, in time, become her 'gods' or heroes, or if negative, her villains or enemies.

Body: There is a natural pigmentation of the skin. Certain areas of the mother's skin darken and thicken, as they protect and prepare her body for labour and lactation. The perineum (the area around the vagina) darkens because of changes which will enable it to stretch during the birth. The areolii (the area around the nipples) darken considerably along with a general increase in pigmentation.

Conflict of Opposites

Soul: This 'thick' skin seems to be in conflict with the pregnant woman's sensitivity and emotional vulnerability. But it forms part of the paradoxical nature of many aspects of pregnancy. Containing the uncontainable, being unstable yet open to change, falling apart yet holding strong, being needy yet able to nurture, the pregnant woman contains within her the conflict of opposites.

At the beginning of pregnancy, then, many major changes are taking place in the mother's body. She will be without her periods and may feel tired and moody, she may suffer from nausea and vomiting (morning sickness) which is said to be a reaction to the increased hormone level and her breasts will swell and tingle. For every physical manifestation of her pregnancy, there are parallel emotional and psychological changes and the interaction of these with external forces such as her history and personal relationships, influence her passage to motherhood.

Not only are women influenced by the physiological and psychological changes their pregnancy brings, there are also social and cultural pressures which in each woman will operate differently, depending on their interaction with her inner world. She will be influenced by her family history and her personal unconscious will be a storehouse of myths and stories relating to pregnancy and birth as handed down to her from her mother and generations of mothers in her family. From her internal mother image she will have conscious and unconscious images of what it is to be a mother. She will have prenatal imprints from her own birth which will be a reflection of her mother's thoughts and feelings during her pregnancy with her and which will influence her in her adaptation to motherhood. Research has shown that the baby in the womb is like a recording machine and all the mother's thoughts and feelings, even words, are recorded and imprinted in the baby's psyche.[3]

The Mother Archetype

Not only, then, is the pregnant woman subject to these more personal influences, she will also be influenced on a deeper level by the mythic images emanating from the collective unconscious of the mother archetype. Conception, pregnancy and giving birth represent an important threshold in the archetypal history of a woman. Jean Shinoda Bolen has written about this aspect of pregnancy:

'While her circumstances make a considerable difference in how a woman feels about being pregnant, if Demeter the mother archetype, is strongly present in her psyche and if her body and spirit have not been desecrated by physical or emotional abuse, then these words of the rosary directed to the Virgin Mary might well fit her experience: "Blessed am I amongst women and blessed is the fruit of my womb." ' Bolen goes on to say that, 'These words are close to voicing the mystical awareness that can arise in women in that moment of revelation when they know that they and the Goddess are one.'[4]

Manuela Dunn Mascetti, in her beautifully illustrated depiction of Goddess mythology describes pregnancy thus:

'. . . the physical phenomenon of pregnancy is almost miraculous in its essence, for woman multiplies herself into another being and becomes the channel for bringing another soul to life. For nine months she creates matter, shapes a body and brings substance within herself like an alchemist transforming essence into living matter.'[5]

Shapes Substance

Archetypes manifest themselves on two levels, collective and personal. On one level they represent a psychological trend of the collective unconscious, a mode of response and behaviour which is universal; on another level, they affect the personal unconscious, bringing to light particular psychological trends in the individual. The way the mother archetype affects a particular woman's psyche will come through symbolically in her dreams, fantasies and moments of intuition and insight. If the mother archetype is wounded perhaps for many generations of mothers in the family, then it is her face that will appear in the dreams of today's pregnant woman.

Pregnancy is a transitional stage and like all transitional phases there will be at this time a re-emergence and reactivation of old conflicts and traumas, particularly those associated with birth and childhood. The pregnant woman may become aware for the first time of unresolved conflicts with her family and her own experience of being mothered will be remembered. If her experiences have not been favourable, she may have a negative mother complex, which will become activated and often will be projected onto her midwife, doctor or another person close to her. Carrying a mother wound which may go as far back as her own birth, she will often seek the positive mother to help her through the transition to motherhood. This will mean that emotional attachments, particularly to those who are involved in her care during pregnancy will become more significant to her at this time.

Initiation

On a deeper level, the pregnant woman is undergoing an archetypal experience. She is undertaking a rite of passage, an initiation. This experience can be compared to that of the Hero in mythology who, in order to be initiated, must undertake a journey into the unknown, or the underworld. Ancient Celts referred to these journeys as *immrama* meaning 'mystical journey', the most famous of which, according to Caitlin Matthews is the voyage of St Brendan. Jungian psychology uses myths and stories from around the world to describe profound psychological processes of change and transformation. The journey of the hero is a metaphor for the journey of the human soul often through tremendous pain and suffering, where what we know has to die in order for a rebirth of the true self to take place. These *immrama's* can be initiated through universal human experiences such as birth and death, loss or separation from a loved one, life-threatening physical illness and so on. At these times, our soul is in danger and usually in profound pain, forcing us to look at our lives in a different way. Often it is through an experience of soul pain that we are propelled into making a journey of self discovery which results in an initiation into higher consciousness or into a greater sense of spiritual fulfilment. Childbirth is one of those experiences which allows us the opportunity for soul growth.

And for all processes of change to happen, there has to be a sacrifice, meaning something always has to die in order for something new to be born. The pregnant woman is in the process of dying to herself as maiden and daughter, in order to give birth to herself as mother. Shinoda-Bolen remarks that the inner pull of pregnancy resembles what happens to people as they are about to die. They become less and less interested in the outside world as they are pulled inwards towards death and the next phase. In letting go of their human form they 'pass on' to another world, just as pregnant women 'pass on' to another stage of their lives.

In undertaking this initiation, women enter the realm of the Mother Goddess and experience one of the sacred woman's mysteries, experiencing what women have experienced since the beginning of time. For many women, the experience of pregnancy and birth may awaken a 'profound sense of kinship with all women throughout history who have ever gone through this ordeal and transformation'.[6]

Fears and Fantasies

Transitional phases are turbulent times; the pregnant woman is in a state of becoming, her body is changing and she is assailed by primitive and archaic fears about herself and the baby inside her. Furthermore, pregnancy is a unique experience in that it is the only time that there are two (or more) people inside one! A pregnant woman's body is not now her sole possession. Something has entered her, taken over her insides and is growing, feeding off her. It is no wonder that pregnant women are prey to all sorts of primitive fears and fantasies.

How will this entity get out? Supposing it grows out of all proportion and the wrong one (meaning herself) is expelled in the birth process? Or, worse still, will her innards be exposed for all to see and what will she produce? Supposing whatever is growing inside is not normal for, in the depth of her night fears, lurks the awful horror that she will produce something weird and too dreadful to be seen. The very idea of something growing inside one and eventually being expelled is strange enough, so how can the mother, who has to take it on trust that it is a real live, normal baby that is growing inside her, be sure?

Raphael-Leff reminds us that the pregnant woman's body is a vessel, whose interior is dark and unknown, even to herself. The growing of a baby in the womb goes on in darkness and there is a mystery about it all. A pregnant woman has inklings of what goes on inside her through books, pictures, hearsay and antenatal scans, but 'she is flooded with horror at the idea of one of her small orifices stretching or being split or cut to let the baby out'[7]

The experience is a universally primitive one and it is common for many women to become aware of all sorts of fears and fantasies during pregnancy. Many of these will find their expression in a wild and active dream life and pregnant women's dreams are unusually crowded with primitive and archaic images. I think that there is generally a lack of awareness and recognition, by not only health carers but society at large, of the primitive, ritualistic and transformative aspect of childbirth. But the reality and depth of the experience speaks otherwise. Every pregnant woman who has ever gone into the delivery room, or experienced a miscarriage induced haemorrhage knows at the very back of her mind, that in the darkest recesses of history, women have died in childbirth and that there is an inherent risk of death (no matter how slight) each time a woman gives birth. Giving birth is a bone deep experience tied to the blood of life.

Pregnancy

Primary Maternal Preoccupation

On a subtle psychological level, there is something else which happens naturally during pregnancy. It is a slight difference in consciousness which allows pregnant women to connect with and to an extent identify with their unborn babies, so that, when the baby is born, the mother will be able to meet its needs. This inner change is called 'Primary Maternal Preoccupation' and was first expounded by D.W. Winnicott.[8] A paediatrician and psychoanalyst with many years of working with mothers and babies, Winnicott has taught us much about the psychological aspects of pregnancy. He contends that there comes about a state in the expectant mother which somewhat alters her state of consciousness to one of heightened sensitivity where she will be able to identify with her baby in order to meet its basic needs. He compares 'primary maternal preoccupation' to a withdrawn or dissociated state and goes so far as to say that it would be an illness were it not for the fact of the pregnancy. It is a state of ego-relatedness between mother and baby, he says, from which the mother will recover and out of which the infant may eventually build the idea of a person in the mother. In less technical language, this means that the mother by virtue of this psychological shift can put herself in her baby's shoes as it were and that this is necessary for the development in the baby of a sense of him or herself. It provides a setting for the infant to begin to grow and develop without having to carry the burdens of life too early on.

I have experienced primary maternal preoccupation in pregnant women as a state of heightened sensitivity and regression, sometimes to more infantile ways of being and thinking. But I also think that it describes another aspect of the inner pull of pregnancy. That it is a necessary precondition to the bonding of mother and baby makes a great deal of sense. That Winnicott in his inherent wisdom and years of observing women and babies, should describe 'primary maternal preoccupation', as a condition which would be an illness were it not for the pregnancy, is vital to understanding the pregnant woman's psyche and what is going on at an inner level, for it explains much about what might otherwise be construed as odd behaviour or intense emotional outbursts in the pregnant woman and the young mother.

Openness

A lowering of normal rational 'coping' mechanisms means an increased vulnerability, but it also means access to other less tangible aspects of life, such as one's spirituality. This is one of the positive aspects of 'primary maternal preoccupation', if one is happy to embrace it, for it means that for a time, we can be less preoccupied with the world outside and we have the ability to connect with other levels of our lives in a way which potentially can enrich it.

Sometimes though, this shift in awareness away from the outer reality of everyday living to the inner world of dreams and fantasy in pregnancy, becomes too sharp and then the mother becomes 'ill' or mentally unstable. It is far from uncommon for women, a few days after they have given birth, to experience altered states of consciousness which may even include hallucinations. This happens most commonly on the third or fourth day after birth and usually coincides with a massive hormonal upheaval in the body of the mother.

Having just given birth, the mother's body needs to adjust to the situation and begins to produce milk to nourish the newborn. It generally takes three days for this to happen, so that the third day is often referred to as the day the milk comes in and the low feelings associated with such a massive change in hormone levels, as the third day blues.

What also happens is that these low feelings follow on from the great high feeling that is common right after giving birth. I remember lying awake all night, exhausted, but being unable to sleep, surveying this wonderful little being that I had produced. Women have told me how, similarly, they were on a high for maybe twenty-four hours after the birth. All this is, I believe, a normal part of the experience of giving birth.

Sometimes, the physical experience of giving birth,

together with the huge hormonal changes in the body and the emotional upheaval of being pregnant one moment and then having a tiny baby to look after the next, can be totally overwhelming. And some new mother's develop puerperal depression, or in more severe cases, psychosis. I have come to the conclusion that in many cases, puerperal psychosis may be the result of primary maternal preoccupation developing into an illness. I think it is highly possible that this happens when it does – that is, after the birth of the baby – simply because, at that time, the containment of pregnancy is gone. In some ways, actually giving birth is to be in a potentially uncontained state. Everything that was previously contained inside is now outside, as it were. Certainly one is very open at that time, not only physically, but emotionally. The preoccupations of pregnancy are no longer appropriate now that the child has been born, so that the mother must make another radical psychological change. Considering the dramatic changes that have occurred and are still occurring in the mother's body immediately after having given birth, it is not surprising that the psyche is also affected.

Primary maternal preoccupation then, manifests as a heightened awareness and an ability to identify with her unborn child on the one level, but outwardly it expresses itself as intense vulnerability, minor regressive behaviour, dreaminess and introverted preoccupation. The pregnant woman may be easily reduced to a child by the medical profession and hospitals and may lose all sense of perspective and objectivity. She is generally extremely sensitive to the suggestions of others and is easily upset by any insensitive treatment or the remarks of health professionals who may be unaware of her vulnerable and precarious state. She may also form attachments to antenatal and birth attendants and project all her hopes of achieving an ideal birth onto those whom she will invest with almost divine powers of transformation.

Primary maternal preoccupation can also be described as a detached state, where the mother withdraws from the outside world and from social interaction. She is less preoccupied by external affairs as she focuses on her baby and what is happening inside her. Indeed, as the pregnancy advances and her physical condition prevents her from pursuing certain activities, she may retreat into a contented, almost lazy and dreamy state of being.

The experience of pregnancy, I believe, leaves no woman untouched. Being pregnant and carrying a child has at once been described as amazing, wonderful, a miracle, frightening, threatening, disgusting, comforting and beautiful. Women report a great many feelings, some of which are paradoxical when they are pregnant and describe the experience, depending on the outcome and circumstances of the particular pregnancy, as the best or the worst time of their lives.

Pregnancy is a multi-faceted state with enormous potential for growth and transformation. Not only is there the possibility of giving birth to a physical baby, there is the potential to give birth to a psychic inner baby, the new mother giving birth to a new part of herself.

Notes

1. For more extensive reading on the physiology of pregnancy see Myles, M. *Textbook For Midwives* (London: Churchill Livingstone, 1989).
2. J. Raphael-Leff *Psychological Processes of Childbearing* (London: Chapman & Hall, 1991).
3. M. Netherton *Past Lives Therapy* (New York: Blum, 1978).
4. J. Shinoda Bolen *Crossing To Avalon* (San Francisco: HarperCollins,1994) p. 57
5. M. Dunn Mascetti *The Song Of Eve* (New York: Fireside Books, 1990) p. 148
6. J. Shinoda Bolen *Crossing To Avalon* p. 61
7. J. Raphael-Leff p. 238
8. D.W. Winnicott *Through Paediatrics to Psychoanalysis* (London: Hogarth Press, 1975).

Prayer Before Birth

I am not yet born; O hear me
Let not the bloodsucking bat or the rat or the stoat or the
clubfooted ghoul come near me.

I am not yet born; console me.
I fear that the human race may with tall walls wall me,
with strong drugs dope me, with wise lies lure me,
on black racks rack me, in blood-baths roll me.

I am not yet born; provide me
With water to dandle me, grass to grow for me, trees to talk
to me, sky to sing to me, birds and a white light
in the back of my mind to guide me.

I am not yet born; forgive me
For the sins that in me the world shall commit, my words
when they speak me, my thoughts when they think me,
my treason engendered by traitors beyond me,
my life when they murder by means of my
hands, my death when they live me.

I am not yet born; rehearse me
In the parts I must play and the cues I must take when
old men lecture me, bureaucrats hector me, mountains
frown at me, lovers laugh at me, the white
waves call me to folly and the desert calls
me to doom and the beggar refuses
my gift and my children curse me.

I am not yet born; O hear me,
Let not the man who is beast or who thinks he is God
come near me.

Louis MacNeice

Chapter Four
I Am Not Yet Born

One imagines that life in the womb is idyllic. It is a safe place where all our needs are catered for without us having to do anything. Our first home is a warm, soft, watery place where we are protected from the demands that life will place on us once we are born. Freud suggested that the prenatal state was characterised by an 'oceanic feeling of bliss' that invoked a wish to return to the womb. Otto Rank, author of *The Trauma of Birth* also held this view. Prenatal life was peaceful and secure so that birth came as a nasty shock to the infant. Womb life was considered to be so wonderful that many people believed we spend the rest of our lives wishing we were back there again.

However, the recent findings of pre- and perinatal psychology suggest that this may not be so. Regression therapy indicates that the womb is also a place where it is possible to suffer and to have experiences which leave deep impressions on our minds. Prenatal life and the way we experience it, has now become a very important part of our continuing lives.

Not so long ago, it used to be thought that the time in the womb did not count. It did not count because mental life began at birth. Unborn babies did not feel, think or dream and life in the womb was irrelevant in a way, as psychological life began at or soon after birth. However, recent studies tell us something quite different. They tell us not only that birth is a crucial, often

traumatic experience for the baby, but also and equally importantly, that the prenatal experience is formative to future life. In
other words, the quality and nature of a child's tenure in the
womb influences not only how he or she will eventually experience birth, but also future life. It also tells us that the fetus and
the unborn baby is not merely a developing biological organism, but a sophisticated evolving human being of immense sensitivity and capability.

**I am not yet born, but I can feel pain and I can react to
my environment. I can dream and even memorise my
experiences in the womb.**

Recent technological advances such as ultrasound, have allowed
us to observe in great detail the fetus and unborn baby in the
womb environment. Extensive research has proved all human
senses to be operative by at least early in the second trimester
(three to six months). The fetus has been shown to be capable
of reactive, as well as spontaneous behaviour and of expressing
distress in various ways. For example, a sixteen week fetus was
observed to react with great spirit to the intrusion into his uterine home of an ultrasound needle, intent on taking fluid from
his spine for tests. As the anaesthetist inserted the needle, the
tiny fetus was seen to strike it with his fist! Another fetus was
seen to withdraw into the corner of the womb, away from the
offending needle.

Unborn babies have a varied repertoire of activities available
to them in the womb. They are capable of spontaneous movements such as daily exercise, swimming around in the amniotic
fluid, sucking their thumbs and scratching their heads. These
are not merely reflexes; the babies choose to do them. At eight
weeks of gestational age, the fetus already enjoys a surprising
degree of mobility and range of movement, showing, moreover,
clear individual initiative and choice of movement.[1]

Unborn babies are exquisitely sensitive to their surroundings in the womb and will move in response to various stimuli
such as its mother's cough or laugh and to intrusions such as

those involved in medical tests. Chamberlain makes the point that 'babies do not live in a fortress but in a mother'.[2] This means that if a mother is emotionally upset, then the baby will be too, as it shares its mothers world of emotion. A fetus whose mother received an electric shock while she was ironing sat bolt upright and immobile in the womb for two days – long after the mother had recovered. Inez Correia has measured the effect on the fetus of a mother viewing brief portions of a violent movie. The fetus was upset as was the mother.[3]

At sixteen weeks, fetal eye movements are observed, with REM sleep seen by twenty weeks, which indicates that unborn babies enjoy a dream life from as early as five months gestational age.

I can hear

The fact that unborn babies can hear comes as no surprise to most mothers, and recent studies indicate that not only can the fetus hear but it is capable of learning and memorising sound. The following French study demonstrates this. Women were asked to relate out loud to their unborn babies (of between thirty three to thirty seven weeks), every evening a fairy story of their choice. Babies not only postnatally showed recognition of the one which was read to them in the womb, but they reacted in utero by a consistent lowering of the heartbeat. Unborn babies can therefore hear and are said to respond well to Brahms and Vivaldi but badly to Wagner and to loud rock music, as one pregnant woman discovered! She had attended a rock concert late in her pregnancy, but had to go home half way through because her unborn baby began to kick vigorously and continued to agitate in protest to the music. When she returned home, she played some Vivaldi and her baby calmed down immediately. The fact that unborn babies can hear is also demonstrated in the way that a newborn recognises not only its mother's voice, but also that of its father. This is particularly the case if the father of the child has been talking to it before birth.

There are many other studies which indicate that unborn babies can learn in the womb.[4]

I can have relationships and I can socialise

It might surprise some readers to know that unborn babies interact socially from very early on. Italian psychoanalyst and author of *From Fetus to Child,* Allesandra Piontelli has contributed greatly to what we know about life in the womb. Her observational study by ultrasound of twins in the womb shows quite clearly that the fetus as early as sixteen weeks is capable of social behaviour. One twin (a boy) was observed to be consistently more active in the uterine environment than his sister who generally slept peacefully curled up in her corner of the womb. Every so often he would wake his sister, by stroking the membrane between them, encouraging her to play. She would wake up and the twins would play together in their mother's womb, moving around behind their respective membranes. They would have gentle boxing matches and tickle one other. Piontelli continued to observe these babies' behaviour after their birth. She found that as toddlers, their favourite game was to play with a curtain between them! They would box and tickle one other, stroking and poking the curtain between them.

David Chamberlain, psychotherapist and author of *Babies Remember Birth* writes of an experiment conducted with premature babies in a special care baby unit. Breathing teddy bears were put in the incubators of a certain number of babies and ordinary teddy bears were placed next to the remainder. The babies who had 'bonded' with the breathing teddy reacted with considerable distress when the bears were taken from them for any length of time, whereas those with the ordinary bears showed no signs of attachment.

Premature babies are babies who should still be in the womb, so it is revealing to note their reactions to such stimuli as breathing teddy bears. Most premature babies will have to spend some time in an incubator, deprived of the warmth of human skin contact except for brief periods when they are changed and some of their physical needs are attended to. The very tiny ones may be fed by tubes so that even feeding will not mean human contact. Whom or what do they bond with? Since we know that they and their siblings still in the womb, are capable of affectionate behaviour, then we must ask ourselves what these little human beings are learning about life and what they are suffering. Those who have worked with premature babies will have observed that they respond extremely well to human contact and obviously feel deprived without it. The midwife who tours the special care baby unit every night, checking each tiny inmate, knows this, as she sees how those who are strong enough have wedged themselves against the wall of their incubator, as though seeking contact with something or someone. A doctor in Brazil proved that premature babies thrive when, instead of spending all their time in incubators, they are carried around kangaroo fashion between the breasts of the midwives!

Researchers in the field of prenatal learning have demonstrated that the fetus learns its mother's diet while still in the womb through the amniotic fluid and this influences its sucking behaviour after birth. This is because the amniotic fluid and mother's breast milk smell the same. This explains why those babies whose mothers have changed their diets before and immediately after birth have much more difficulty establishing breast-feeding than those mothers whose diets remain unchanged. The ability of the fetus to learn in the womb has evolved as an essential tool for its life after birth and ensures that when it is time to be born the baby is equipped to survive in its new environment.

Within the psychoanalytic profession, it has come to be thought that a child's sense of self may begin prior to birth. Piontelli's work indicates that there is continuity of behaviour between prenatal and postnatal life. What is also important is that her observations show clearly how events in the womb, such as a threatened miscarriage, severely affect the fetus and are responsible for reactive behaviour well into postnatal life.

This indicates something which may seem perfectly obvious to prenatal psychologists and to mothers: that babies have a memory and that experiences in the womb are recorded somewhere in the unconscious mind.

Piontelli demonstrates this through the story of a little girl named Pina. Piontelli observed Pina through ultrasound scan, from sixteen weeks of gestational age, every four weeks to birth and to three years of age. At the first two observations, Pina could be seen to be actively exploring her uterine environment; she moved a lot and was extremely active in the womb. Shortly after the second ultrasound observation, in which Pina was seen to play with and pull on the placenta, Pina's mother suffered a near miscarriage because of a partial detachment of the placenta. She was made to take complete rest and the miscarriage was averted, but the effect on Pina was dramatic. When next observed, four weeks later, Pina was curled up tightly in the corner of the womb, immobile. She remained so for almost the remainder of the pregnancy and at delivery (which was by caesarean section) was found to be deeply lodged in the womb and difficult to 'get out'.

In postnatal observations, Pina's behaviour indicated a pattern of active, almost manic exploration of her environment, followed by anxieties often of a claustrophobic nature which rendered her immobile and fearful. Her mother was reported as saying that Pina was especially terrified of water and hated being washed. Pina would cling to the side of her baby bath and scream as her mother tried to wash her: 'It was as if she were afraid of being washed away.' The experience of the near fatal miscarriage seems to have affected Pina so that she carried it with her as an unconscious memory and it undoubtedly coloured and influenced her postnatal behaviour.

Thomas Vernay, author of *The Secret life of the Unborn Child*, and other workers in the field of regression therapy, claim that what happens in the womb and at birth will affect how the adult will handle stressful situations in later life. The findings of hypnotherapists have suggested that the fetus records all the mother's thoughts and even everything said to her, by her and in her presence, as if it applied to him.[5] The fetus has no ego, that is, it has no discriminatory capacity and so it takes on its mother's thoughts and feelings as though they are its own. Thus, adults in therapy can discover that they are unconsciously carrying emotional imprints which may have originated in their mother's experiences during pregnancy. In therapy, it is possible to perceive the chains of experience that span generations and to hear in the voices of adult babies, their mother's and even their father's stories. The sum of this work suggests that the unborn child is profoundly affected by its prenatal awareness.

Arthur Janov, the founder of primal therapy, writes about very negative experiences in the womb, saying that for many babies, life in the womb can be a nightmare from which the child is helpless. He suggests that research indicates that mothers unhappy about their pregnancies produce babies who are irritable and restless, who cry excessively, eat poorly and vomit frequently. We know that every cell in the baby's body is nourished out of the mother's body, which means that what affects the mother will affect the baby. Most substances taken by the mother will cross the placenta, however filtered. Furthermore, what happens during the nine months of pregnancy often foretells the quality of the subsequent mother-child relationship. Current thinking now claims that being ignored or resented in the womb is communicated through an adverse chemical reaction and that this is usually compounded after birth by more inattention towards and resentment of the child by the mother. This means that rejection and emotional deprivation may begin in the womb.

Dibs

Janov uses the story of Dibs to movingly illustrate this. He says that Dibs is a clear, resounding answer to our question of whether a child can suffer in the womb[6]. Some readers may be familiar with the story of Dibs, a child diagnosed as autistic and mentally retarded, who came to be treated by psychotherapist Virginia Axeline. The therapist interviewed Dibs' parents as part of her treatment and it became clear that Dibs' mother had never wanted to become pregnant and had resented her baby through-out her difficult pregnancy. This continued through the birth and into Dibs' early childhood. He upset all his parents plans and her career as a surgeon. He was big and ugly at birth and it soon became apparent that he was not normal. His parents took him to see a psychiatrist when he was five and it was he who told them that Dibs was not mentally defective or psychotic or brain-damaged, but the most rejected and emotionally deprived child he had ever seen. This mentally handicapped child had a mea-sure IQ of 168 at the age of six and his reading age exceeded what was normal for his age by several years. Dibs appears to be a case of severe prenatal suffering.

There are many other such stories and the idea that a baby can suffer in the womb is now an accepted fact. Babies have been born seemingly rejecting their mothers by refusing to feed, or developing allergic reactions to breast milk. Perhaps these infants are expressing something about the nature of their emotional experiences in the womb. Janov asserts that a child is not born naturally rejecting its mother unless it has a history of hurt, a hurt derived from rejection transmitted in the womb.

There is no doubt that life in the womb can also be idyllic. Unborn babies are as much affected by positive stimuli and the security of feeling loved and wanted by their mothers as they are by negative feelings. It is the only time in our lives when we will be contained in this way and the Freudian notion of intrauterine bliss has some foundation. In my own work I have found that there were times when real healing began in the wounded individual when we reached the prenatal level of awareness. A woman who felt herself to be unloved and who could find little or no comfort in returning to the feelings of her childhood, was profoundly touched when she remembered that her sick mother had spent many months of her pregnancy afraid to move in case she lost her child. The awareness that she had been so precious to her mother released in her profound feelings of love. I remember the moment well. It was as though something shifted and clicked into place. It felt permanent and unshakeable. No matter how badly she might feel, she could always return to this place where she had *experienced* being loved.

So, though not yet born, the child is a feeling, sensing being of immense capability and sensitivity, who will, by the time of birth, have enjoyed a variety of experiences in the womb, some good and some bad. These experiences will influence how the child will go on to live that life outside the womb. A look at prenatal life helps us to get a sense of how it might be for the baby to be born, because it is likely that the baby's prenatal awareness, together with their experiences in the womb, have an influence on how they will experience birth. What is certain is that labour and birth are a tremendous struggle, for many of us the closest we may ever come to death. There is little doubt that it is painful, that it is an ordeal and that it is an overwhelming experience, even when it occurs naturally.

Notes

1. de Vries et al. (1988) and Ianniruberto, A. and Tajani, E. (1981) Ultrasonographic study of fetal movements. *Seminars in Perinatology*, 5 (2).
2. Chamberlain, D. Presidential Address APPPAH 7th International Congress (1995) in *Pre- and Perinatal Psychology Jrn.* 10 (2).
3. Corria (1994) quoted in above.
4. Blum, T. (ed.) Prenatal perception, learning and bonding (1993). Berlin: Leonardo Publishers.
5. M. Netherton see above, p. 125.
6. A. Janov Imprints: *The Lifelong Effects of The Birth Experience.* (Coward/Mc Cann, 1983), p. 3.

Chapter Five

Giving Birth

It was hot and stuffy in the labour room. Glancing over at Betty who lay dozing on the bed, I pulled aside the curtain and peered outside at the grey darkness. It was three thirty in the morning and we had been there nearly twenty hours. John, his face lined with exhaustion, had gone to catch some sleep in a nearby room. I sighed and closed my eyes; they felt tired and gritty. Betty had been in labour all day. She lay there, an exhausted heap, neatly belted up to the labour monitor, her epidural dulling her senses enough for her to get some rest.

'You are very slow' the midwife had said. Midwife number two, that was; we were now on midwife number three. In a few hours we would possibly be back to number one again. I wondered what she would say when she saw us, a sorry looking trio, nothing like the bright and eager lot of yesterday. Betty was progressing well then: three centimetres dilated on admission and getting strong contractions. Twenty minutes in the labour room and her waters had broken, surely a promising start. But regretfully, here we were and Betty, who by now had been examined by no fewer than five different people at regular intervals, was pronounced to be making very little progress. Each new doctor was greeted eagerly: what news do you have for us our eyes asked, but the looks on their faces as they pulled off their obstetric gloves and washed their hands was always the

59

same. Nodding slightly, 'Not much change, we'll give it another couple of hours', they said and left.

The young midwife was busy writing her notes. It was clear that no one held out much hope that Betty could avoid a caesarean. Betty herself, though exhausted, searched my face for hope. I felt heavy with the weight of it. 'Oh God, don't desert us', I cried inwardly with a silent prayer. Summoning up all my strength, I managed to say to her, 'you must believe in yourself; you can do it.' I believed even then that she could, but dulled with tiredness and the haze of negative emotion, I was finding it difficult to be, as it seemed, the sole carrier of this hope. 'Keep positive', I repeated, as much to myself as to anyone else. John had already crumbled under the strain. The stress and worry was very difficult for him. And it was taking so long. Seeing Betty in pain and feeling powerless to help her had overwhelmed him. He could not cope. Betty, sensing this, aggravated the situation by clinging to me desperately, frantic to keep me in the room. I knew that she saw me as her capable, strong part, the one who could help her do it.

Enter doctor number three. The sound of her voice jerked me into instant alertness. Even Betty was suddenly awake. Something in the doctor's voice had caught our attention.

'What are you doing here?' she asked. 'Come on, let's have a look. Let's see if you can have this baby by the time I go off duty.' Suddenly the atmosphere in the room changed. This woman exuded a new hope, something different. I snapped to attention, whispering a silent thank you. Examining Betty, the doctor pushed and pulled a little, her fingers making space, making room inside Betty's body for the baby to come. All of us held our breath and waited. The strain became unbearable.

'Six centimetres. Let's see if we can get it to seven' she said.

Someone said later, 'Oh she's called Dr magic fingers!' I can see why, I thought.

The examination, though uncomfortable, seemed to perk Betty up and she was helped into an upright posture. Sitting up, standing, kneeling or squatting in labour is very beneficial, as it elicits the help of gravity, particularly for the final stages.

'I'll be back in two hours and you'll be ready to push that baby out then OK?'

She breezed out. She was beautiful I thought; I wished she could have stayed. But her positive energy stayed with us and from then on we never looked back. We struggled through another two hours and again held our breath in anticipation as poor Betty was re-examined. This time she was pronounced to be progressing well and there was no longer any talk of caesareans. Betty, though pleased that things seemed to be happening faster now, was too exhausted and bruised to take an active part. As the anaesthetic effects of the epidural began to wear off, she started to protest as waves of pain swept over her. Tired also, I forced myself into action and took her through her breathing routine, trying to help her concentrate. Luckily the epidural was only a partial one, which allowed a degree of movement, so with John and I supporting her, Betty began to walk around the room, pausing to breathe through the contractions which were coming with more intensity. She began to cry.

'I can't stand it anymore, I can't do it.'

'Yes you can. Keep going. You can do it,' I urged. John joined his voice to mine and held her reassuringly. The midwife, alerted by Betty's cries, calls the doctor and Betty is helped back to the bed. The baby needs constant monitoring and we must not exceed the limit of the belts which connect Betty to the monitor. If we go too far away from the bed, then it ceases to function. Although the doctors had agreed to take it off for a few moments, concern about the baby meant almost constant screening.

One and a half hours later Betty kneels over the end of the bed and pushes her son out herself. She clings to John and they cry as their son is handed to them. I hold back, aware that the new family must be allowed to bond undisturbed. I thank God again and, lying in the back of the cab on the way home, I sigh, a contented sigh this·time. The contented sigh of a job well done.

Approaching the Birth: Fears And Fantasies

The pregnant woman, having carried her baby for nine months, now approaches the birth with anticipation and, most certainly with mixed feelings. She eagerly awaits her first meeting with her baby, but her eagerness is tinged with anxieties and apprehensions about the birth itself. She may be assailed by all sorts of the most primitive fears and fantasies, for deep inside her she wonders how this baby will be born. And particularly if this is her first experience of giving birth, she wonders how she will cope with the pain which at some deep level she fears will take her to the limits of her endurance and maybe even well beyond it. Will she lose control of herself? Will she howl for help, unable to bear the agony? Will she be split open, her body torn apart by the emerging force inside her pushing to be born? And worst of all, supposing something should go wrong and the baby gets stuck, what will happen then? Will the child be torn from her with heavy instruments invading and cutting into her private parts, tearing at her flesh, like a confession wrenched from a torture victim? Or further even, if that should fail, will she be wheeled into the operating theatre and anaesthetised, her body cut open to remove the baby, leaving her lying there, her body an empty shell. And she might even die, never waking up from the anaesthetic. And, even if she does, what will come out of her? Supposing 'it' is malformed, a monster, too awful to be looked at? And in her wildest most archaic thoughts lurks the fear of being exposed from the inside as she wonders what else will be extracted from her along with the baby.

Not every pregnant woman will think all these things, but many will at some primitive level, especially in the dark hours of the night. The perhaps irrational fear of dying during childbirth is not so difficult to understand, given the nature of the experience. Not so long ago, it happened that women died giving birth to their babies. Nowadays it is a rare occurrence of course, but our souls, our inner mother still remembers. This is because giving birth is such an instinctive and primitive act of nature rooted in our history. And at a symbolic level, women do die when they give birth. A part of them dies in order to give birth to new life.

Of course a pregnant woman will also think about the more positive aspects of her impending labour. She is glad that the period of waiting is nearly over. She is glad that the nine months during which she has been patient, carrying her baby under her heart, nurturing and protecting it, is almost over and she will be rewarded when finally, joyously, she will first set eyes on her child. She wonders what it will look like, this child inside her, whom she already knows so well and who has been her constant companion for nine months. This baby she has imagined a thousand times, will it be as she has pictured it? Many times she has played the fantasy right to the end: the labour, the birth and finally, the magical moment when she falls in love with he or she whom she has carried inside her for so long. She imagines it and as she does, she is filled with wonder at the miracle of it all. She is filled with joy and peace as inside her mind, sacred images of the Madonna and child merge with those of her and her baby.

And what of her labour, what of the birth? Many times she has rehearsed the scene, many times she has gone over her preparations. She feels she is well prepared and hopes that it will be a fulfilling experience, that she will feel empowered by it and afterwards revel in her success. After all, she has achieved this most wonderful thing. She has fashioned this new being inside her like an alchemist transforming essence into living matter. When her baby is born, she will bask in her new-found status of mother; she will be transformed, no longer simply a woman, but a woman blest with her child.

Each woman will deal with the final stages of pregnancy and its accompanying emotions, fantasies and expectations in a manner particular to her and each woman, imbued with her own influences and armed with her own brand of techniques, will face the prospect of labour and delivery of her baby in her own way. For many, it is a journey into the unknown, for others a path well-worn, though always open to the unexpected. Each labour and birth experience is different. Other influences, external ones beyond the woman's control, will interact with her own, so that the experience will always be a fresh one, though the outcome may be predictable. There are many different types of labour and births, but what is important ultimately is how the process is experienced by the mother and her baby.

Social and cultural influences play a very important part in how an individual pregnant woman approaches the birth of her baby. In a society dominated by patriarchal values, which places childbirth in the hands of the medical profession rather than the women themselves, many women will simply distance themselves from the experience and hope for the best, placing their trust in the doctors. Taught that having a baby is a painful and hazardous ordeal to be conducted in a hospital, the pregnant woman may resign herself to the inevitable. She may set aside her own potential to give birth and surrender to the ministrations of the 'professionals', believing that they know best and knowing that if the pain gets too much, she can be anaesthetised or, better still, she can have the epidural right away before contractions begin to really hurt.

Instinctual Natures

Those women who may feel more strongly connected to their own instinctual natures will approach childbirth differently. Many will choose a particular type of antenatal preparation which will enhance their own innate capabilities to give birth and enable them to approach the birth with confidence. For those who choose this way, the path is far from easy. Preparing for labour and birth is one thing, getting the kind of birth you want is quite another. Although these classes are designed to help women give birth, they (the classes) will usually have to contend with the particular dictates of the obstetric system and may even inadvertently cause difficulties for the pregnant woman. This is especially so when the woman prepares for a natural birth, but finds too late, that the hospital advocates medical management of labour.

Giving Birth

Suffice it to say that the way in which a pregnant woman has prepared for her labour and the birth of her baby, will also influence the way she experiences it. At a profound level, I believe that women want to experience the birth of their children as positive and fulfilling. They wish, sometimes unconsciously, to be affirmed or confirmed in their own ability to give birth; they want to be empowered by their experience of childbirth.

No woman remains untouched by childbirth; it is an experience of enormous proportions. It will most certainly change her life and what happens and how she feels about the experience will affect her transition into motherhood and her early relationship with her baby. It is a strange fact that relatively little emphasis has been placed on the mother's experience. This is despite the fact that we are becoming increasingly more aware of the significance of the birth experience to future life. Psychology and particularly psychoanalysis, has been slow to accept that not only is the prenatal and birth experience formative, but that since mother and child are fundamentally interconnected, all the mother's thoughts and feelings have an impact on her child. This is now an accepted point of view. With this in mind, it is particularly important that we begin to look at the mother's experience of giving birth, with a view to ameliorating the conditions under which women are asked to bring their children into the world.

When we speak of the birth trauma, we are generally thinking of the experience of the baby. And though not as much has been written about the birth experience from the mother's point of view, I have found that the word trauma can also be used to describe what some women experience during their baby's birth. Of course not all women experience giving birth as traumatic, although there can be disturbing elements depending on the kind of birth a woman has. Even a 'normal' birth (that is one without medical intervention) can be subjectively experienced as deeply upsetting. This is particularly true for the wounded, or unsupported mother, who may find it more difficult to cope with the overwhelming nature of the experience.

The reality of our modern society means that most women will be offered a medicalised approach to prenatal and birth care. Years of working with pregnant and postnatal women, as well as my own birth experiences, have led me to form certain conclusions about the way in which women experience the birth of their babies. If the birth is 'mechanised', that is, if there has been medical intervention, women almost always experience some degree of shock depending on the type of intervention. For example, a forceps delivery is very often associated with being 'violated' or even raped. The use of instruments to deliver the baby may be equated with violence. A caesarian birth will often be associated with feelings of loss and incompleteness. This means that giving birth becomes a deeply wounding experience, as opposed to a joyful and fulfilling one.

Having a difficult birth experience does not preclude feelings of delight at the arrival of the new baby, but often this is marred by a sense of being wounded both physically and emotionally. And the depth of the wound means the soul has been touched and hurt. Difficulties often arise because, as a result of feelings of guilt or maybe even of rage, the new mother may be unable to fully bond with her baby or experience its joyful nature. If any of us are wounded, we react and it is part of being human that we form defences against the pain of injury, be it at a physical or a soul level.

Psychological defences against this type of birth experience are similar to those of any traumatic occurrence and involve numbness and a kind of 'cutting out.' Cutting out is a defence mechanism employed by the ego when a trauma is too great to be borne. As such it is a survival mechanism and protects the person from an experience of pain which is considered unbearable. You can usually tell a woman who has been through a distressing labour and birth experience. For a few days, weeks, or even months, she will have a shocked, dazed, faraway expression on her face. She may describe this feeling as light headedness, or fuzziness. Though the physical practicalities of looking after a newborn will usually come naturally, the shocked mother's actions will appear as though automatic. If we are preoccupied or depressed, we will often perform our life functions as though we are on automatic, but our actions are empty, for part of us is missing. These are all expressions of being slightly ungrounded or out of body, a common reaction to trauma or shock.

Splitting

Another common type of psychological defence against traumatic experience involves 'splitting', which can be described as separating experiences from each other. An example of this is the mother who has a difficult birth in which medical or surgical intervention is involved and who feels so violated by the experience that she blames the medical establishment and does not think of her own wound. This type of experience most often leaves women feeling victimised by the medical profession. And when one identifies with the victim position, then one becomes a prisoner of one's own helplessness. It means that becoming aware of one's own experience is not possible.

What happens in a therapy situation is that the mother will begin to become aware of her own feelings, such as repressed anger. This releases her from her former position as victim and enables a potential healing to take place. 'Splitting' as a mechanism of psychological defence makes it difficult for a true healing to take place in the individual. Uncovering our own vulnerability and the pain of being humiliated in our most intimate core will enable the experience to somehow come together and for a healing to take place.

Feeling Disempowered

Feeling 'disempowered' or disabled is another very common response to very medicalised and forceps births. This means that the mother feels that she was unable to give birth to her child and that the baby was extracted from her. The pain of being wounded in this way can be very deep and can touch on many other painful layers in the heart of the new mother. Jackie's story tells us something of the nature of this wound.

Songs From The Womb

Jackie

Jackie came to me for postnatal counselling, after attending antenatal classes before the birth of her son, Chris. In her thirties, she was a mature and sensitive woman who had embarked late on motherhood. She and her husband had planned the baby and welcomed his arrival. Though possessed of a natural gentleness through which it was possible to glimpse her vulnerability, she appeared strong and self-contained in the group and she mixed well with the other women. She looked forward to the birth and whilst preparing for what she hoped would be a normal birth, she was not unduly rigid about how that should happen.

Nonetheless, her labour and the birth of her son, fell far short of what she had been expecting and caused her profound pain. At full term, she was induced with oxytocin (a labour-inducing drug) and after a long and painful labour, with fetal distress developing in second stage, Chris was born by the use of forceps. It was said by the medical attendants at that time that Jackie's contractions were insufficient and that she was unable to push her baby out herself. Jackie experienced the birth as traumatic, particularly the forceps delivery.

A few weeks after the birth she came to the postnatal group, but asked me if I would see her privately for counselling. I was not surprised and was glad that she had suggested this, for I was shocked at how she looked. No longer happy with the softness and glow of pregnancy, she seemed instead sad and distraught. Though there was no question that she loved her baby son, what should have been a joyous experience had turned out to be a disturbing one. Jackie was a naturally warm person and it was clear to me that she had been hurt very deeply and that she badly needed to talk about her experience.

In the sessions Jackie 'relived' the birth a number of times, always becoming very distressed as she did so. She needed to recount her birth story over and over again and for me to listen to it. She felt that Chris had been 'taken from her', removed from her body and that *she* had not been able to give birth to

68

him. She felt disconnected from the birth and from something which she and her child should have shared.

'We were not able to work together,' she said.

Worst of all and compounding the pain she felt about the manner in which the birth had taken place, was her sense of guilt that Chris had been subjected to the harsh violence of the forceps. This was very painful for her and threw up all her old feelings of not being good enough. Jackie had been in analysis before and had worked on this aspect of her feelings, but giving birth had reactivated old wounds. In addition to her feeling of guilt at not having.been able to give birth to Chris herself, Jackie experienced the forceps birth as personally disempowering and humiliating. Furthermore, the experience left her feeling violated. This was painfully illustrated by a dream which Jackie recounted in the first session.

There are two men fixing the roof of my house. They are rough workmen and I bring Chris up to them to show him off. One of the men says 'May I hold him?' 'Yes' I answer and hand Chris to him. The workman holds the baby and then asks, 'Can my mate hold him?' He is a stern looking man, but Chris is passed to him. I turn away, chatting to the first man. Then I hear Chris whimper. I turn round suddenly to take the baby and when he is placed in my arms I see that the man has put his eyes out.

The two workmen represent the doctors who delivered Chris. That they were rough workmen is how Jackie's unconscious experienced them. Workmen fixing the roof of her house is symbolic of her vulnerability and sense of being physically open and unprotected during her son's birth. That one of them puts Chris's eyes out is symbolic of a deep wound to the soul. Eyes are often called mirrors of the soul and from the Oedipus myth, we learn that eye gouging is also symbolic of psychological castration, for when Oedipus learns of his crime, he is so appalled that he puts his own eyes out and is thus condemned to a life of blind wandering. In Jackie's dream, when her baby is returned to her, he has been blinded. The dream image is very specific and shows us clearly that not only had Jackie been deeply wounded by her experience of giving birth, but also that she perceived how wounding it had been for her child to be born in this way.

Wounding

The dream, which came shortly after the birth and had been recurrent since then, ceased as a result of the therapy, for dreams are the soul's way of speaking to us when we are so wounded that we cannot see. By listening to and telling our dreams to someone else, we discover our inside stories. And when we have learnt the story of the soul, then it ceases to plague us by recurrent dreams or symptoms.

Jackie's dream and her feelings about it, are a common reaction to a birth in which forceps have been used to deliver the baby. Being unable to push her baby out herself leaves the mother feeling incomplete. She feels that her body has let her down and, worse, that she has let her baby down. Although she is relieved to have her baby extracted from her, she nonetheless often experiences the forceps delivery as an attack. At this vulnerable time the instruments can assume the proportions of torture implements and many women report feeling distressed and frightened.

'I was trying to be really grown up and helpful, but when they broke the waters I just lost my mind. The contractions suddenly came non-stop and I had no chance to catch up and adjust to the excruciating waves of pain. I panicked and just could not stop screaming and then when the baby got stuck I heard them say "Get the forceps, cut her!" It felt like an attack. Afterwards there was blood everywhere as if a murder had taken place.'[1]

An instrumental delivery will often trigger memories of past sexual or physical abuse, the 'violated' woman frequently projecting all her rage onto the doctors or midwives responsible for brutally wrenching her baby from her. One woman referred to the doctor as 'that butcher with blood on his hands.' The reality of forceps delivery is not very pleasant. The labouring woman is usually 'tied' down on the bed, with her legs wide apart and bound to stirrups to prevent her struggling. There may be two or more people peering between her legs and one of them will be inside her with sharp instruments pulling her baby out. Often, the woman will be so frightened and in pain that she will be screaming as her child is pulled out of her. Anyone who has seen a forceps delivery can vouchsafe for the high degree of force that is needed to drag out the baby. One husband described it as 'a torture scene', and felt so distressed by his wife's screams and the procedure that he said he never wanted to have another child. Women have told me that they felt as if their insides were being pulled out.

These are dramatic experiences which may leave deep scars on both the mother and her baby. While delivering a baby with the use of forceps may be necessary in certain conditions, often the way in which this procedure is carried out adds to the depth of the trauma. Sensitivity on the part of the doctors and birth attendants to the experience of both the mother and her baby will help to mitigate some of its effects.

It is often difficult for the mother who feels inadequate because she has had to succumb to an instrumental delivery, to express her feelings of rage, anger and deep emotional pain. What happens, then, is that the wounded mother may transfer her feelings about herself onto the baby, to whom she now becomes a 'therapist', wanting to make reparation for the damage she feels has been caused to her child. She will then constantly cosset the baby in an attempt to both alleviate her guilt at not being a good enough mother and to repair the psychological damage she fears has been caused to her child.[2] In effect, this means that the baby is now the carrier of his or her mother's wounded self and becomes referred to as 'poor baby.' The awful birth is then something the baby (and not the mother) has experienced and been fractured by, because the deeply wounded mother projects her pain and sense of irretrievable damage onto her child.

In addition, she may harbour feelings of guilt and even shame relating to the experience, for which at some deep level she feels she is to blame. She has not been a good enough mother. Unable to give birth to her baby herself, she is a failure. Feelings like this will be exacerbated by remarks made by the medical attendants at her labour. Phrases such as 'failure to progress' and 'poor maternal effort', though accepted medical jargon, are hurtful and patronising.

Sometimes we fail to recognise that when we are wounded, even words can hurt.

Caesarean Section

Having a baby by caesarean section has certain psychological implications for both the mother and her baby. That said, there needs to be a distinction between labour caesarean and non-labour caesarean. Non-labour caesareans are usually planned. These include women who may have prepared for a normal vaginal delivery and who discover later in their pregnancies that for one reason or another they will be unable to give birth naturally and who therefore have time to prepare themselves for the operation. Furthermore, it is unusual for the mother in this case to go into labour since the caesarean operation is done either before or at term.

Labour caesareans, on the other hand, are usually an emergency and involve those women who have had normal pregnancies and for whom complications arise during labour. In most cases this is an emergency procedure to deliver the baby safely after an unsuccessful attempt at normal delivery. The significance of this is that women will have experienced labour or contractions *before* the caesarean is performed, a fact which will also affect the unborn child. In some cases, an emergency caesarean will be performed before labour if a potentially life-threatening situation develops for either the mother or the baby or both. This may take place for example when a maternal haemorrhage due to placenta previa occurs, which is the technical term for when the placenta is lying over the neck of the womb.

For many women, birth by caesarean section is traumatic, particularly if it is an emergency. A caesarean is a major operation, a surgical intervention, which in many cases is performed to save the baby's life and occasionally, the mother's. But pregnancy is a process, however, not a condition and birth is the culmination of that process.[3] Birth by caesarean section, however imperative, is a dramatic interruption of that process and, although at times necessary, it can be experienced by both mother and baby as a violent act of separation. The feelings involved are similar to the abrupt ending of a relationship. Such an ending feels incomplete because neither party has had time to come to terms with the ending, however inevitable, for emotional separation involves a gradual process of detachment. By its very nature (a caesarean section takes between ten and twenty-five minutes), it is violent and sudden, allowing no time for adaptation, as does the course of normal labour which lasts for much longer (a matter of hours or even days). The human organism is shocked. It happens and it is over.

Incompleteness

Stories from some of my clients who have had caesarean sections have illustrated reactions to this sudden interruption. Most of these women experienced incompleteness in some way or the other. Arlene said: 'I haven't been through the process. I feel like me and my baby were forcibly separated.' Liz: 'After the operation they showed me my baby. It was strange, I didn't feel that he really belonged to me.'

This reaction of doubting that the baby is really hers may appear irrational, but it is entirely understandable in the circumstances. For something to happen and be acknowledged, there has to be an awareness of it. Women who are delivered of their babies by caesarean section under a general anaesthetic are particularly prone to this form of reaction, since they are 'asleep' during the birth. They 'wake up' to motherhood.[4] The result is often this struggle to feel part of the experience and to thus bond with their newborns to whom they have not actively given birth. A labour and birth ordeal of this sort is difficult for the new mother to assimilate and some women experience a detachment both from themselves and their babies and say they do not feel part of the experience and have difficulty bonding to their babies immediately.

This was painfully illustrated in Belinda's case: 'One minute I was in the labour room trying to push my baby out and the next I was lying semi-conscious and someone was showing me this bundle whom they said was my baby. I didn't see him being born. I feel as if I wasn't there when he was born.'

One young mother who ended up with a caesarean section after a long, protracted labour, was found later roaming the wards, tears running down her cheeks, asking, 'Did you see my baby being born?' Every midwife she met was asked the same question until eventually she spoke with the actual midwife who had assisted at the operation. The young mother questioned her again and again, as if by doing so each detail of the precious experience which had been denied her would be indelibly imprinted in her soul and the experience restored to her.

Many women have told me how important it was for them to actually feel or see their baby emerging from their bodies. Not being able to do this resulted for some in tremendous pain and loss, feelings of unreality and detachment and most commonly a sense of something missing.

Although we are unlikely to be able to obliterate the need for caesarean section births, awareness of the psychological implications, as well as the sensitivities of the mother and her baby, should encourage better handling of this important event. A recognition of the emotional effects of surgical intervention on the experience of birth, would enable the procedure to be conducted as humanely as possible, with special regard for the sanctity of birth and the importance of bonding between mother and child.

Women are affected in various ways by caesarean births and common negative and emotionally painful reactions should not be denied or minimalised. Separation of mother and baby at a time when it is crucial that they be together is compounded by the mother's reaction of detachment from a baby she has difficulty believing came from her. All this means that the earliest relationship between mother and baby may be fraught with difficulties because it may take some time for the wounded mother to begin to love her baby. Many women who have had their babies by caesarean feel that there is something missing. Others feel cheated out of something and some feel profoundly depressed, but are unable to say why.

Wounded Feminine Pride

Even more devastatingly, deep feelings of insecurity and negative self-image are common, as the mother blames herself for being unable to do what other women do so naturally. Women often unconsciously see giving birth as a test of their womanhood and so women whose babies are delivered by caesarean section (and often, forceps) can suffer from a negative self/body image, since they feel their bodies were unable to function normally. Such women carry a sense of wounded feminine pride. I have worked with many a wounded mother who carries a profound sense of guilt, that in some way she has deprived her child of the experience of normal birth, something which many consider to be a birthright. Guilty at having inflicted pain on her baby, she punishes herself and her body, which has let her down so badly. In some women, a caesarean section and instrumental birth produce postnatal depression. Again, the mother's experience of childbirth is often overlooked as a possible cause or even a contributing factor to postnatal depression. This is surely a mistake, for I believe the way the postnatal mother has experienced childbirth is a major factor in postnatal illness.

The trauma of this birth experience can be further compounded when it involves a sense of having been violated by health professionals whom, it is sometimes felt, artificially intervene in the natural process. It is not unusual for women to report feeling that they were prevented from giving birth naturally. If a woman feels that, then she carries resentment in her heart for some time afterwards and the birth of her child is tainted with the brush of betrayal. And it is this very resentment which will often propel her headlong into another pregnancy in a compulsive effort to 'get it right this time'.

Depression

Thus, we have a mother, wounded in the very core of her being, so depressed and dejected it is often difficult for her to bond with her baby, who feels to her like a stranger and to whom she did not actively give birth. The bonding difficulties can have severe repercussions on the baby and the mother-baby relationship itself, because the mother may also blame the baby for her bad experience and project all her negativity onto her child, who then becomes the cause of all her troubles.

This is not so difficult to understand if we look at the following post birth situation. The new mother feels disappointed and physically low after a difficult birth; she feels violated and deeply wounded and she may also be battling with a sense of guilt and failure that she has not been able to give birth naturally. She has difficulty bonding with a baby who seems like a stranger; she feels disconnected from her baby and therefore from part of herself. She may blame herself, the baby and/or the medical staff. Try as she might, she cannot respond to this child, who is a constant reminder of the ordeal she has had to endure. She feels guilty that she should feel so bad about the experience; after all, she has a healthy baby, so what has she got to be so miserable about? She fears that no one will understand her feelings; she is in mourning for something, she is not sure what. She is grieving for the loss of her ideal birth. Feeling that she will not be understood, she turns inwards into her pain and sense of shame; she becomes depressed and unable to cope, which in turn causes more guilt and she develops postnatal depression.

Depression after the birth of a child will mean a disturbed early life experience for the baby and profound pain and psychological suffering for the mother, for if a mother is hurting badly, then it can be difficult for her to see and love her child.

Studies have shown that there is a higher incidence of child abuse in families where there has been caesarean birth.[5] This appeared to be the case with Linda, a young woman who felt herself to be emotionally deprived and who was born by emergency caesarean section. Linda felt that her mother always had a 'down' on her and that this was as a direct result of her birth experience. At some far from conscious level, it felt as though Linda's mother had never been able to forgive her child for the pain her birth had caused. Linda internalised this, growing up with the unconscious message that, since her coming into existence had been the cause of so much pain, she must be bad, or there must be something wrong with her.

I have found in my clinical work that this type of birth and early life experience often activates in the personality of the individual, a kind of sacrificial or martyr tendency. The person seems to need to atone for some wrongdoing. Perhaps this has to do with feelings of guilt and a need to constantly make up for having been the cause of so much pain at their birth. If coming into life means pain to the one who is bringing you into life, then perhaps it makes it hard to feel positive about living. Or it may feel like one has to continually atone for being alive.

Getting It Right

In my experience, the vast majority of women who have had caesarean section births, are desperate to have a normal birth the next time. I have come to realise that this need to 'get it right' can often be a repetition compulsion, because the mother feels compelled to repeat the experience in an unconscious effort to heal the old one. For some it will mean that having a natural birth becomes vital, but painfully, they are told that their chances of doing so are substantially reduced. Women with an already low self-image are given a 'trial of scar', which in obstetric terminology means a trial of labour. There is a small risk that the uterus may not be able to sustain the contractions of labour and may rupture because of the scarring of the previous caesarean. In most cases, though, given good support, many women can go on to have normal vaginal births and if they do, it is generally with a great sense of relief and fulfilment.

Premature Birth

Pre-term labour abruptly curtails pregnancy before the mother and her unborn baby have had time to emotionally begin to separate. The mother is unprepared for the birth and if this takes place in a state of crisis, she is most likely 'in shock.' The birth of a premature baby will have its own special difficulties. One of these is with loving. When the survival of the baby is unsure (as in Linda's case), many parents will protect themselves from falling in love with the baby, while unconsciously preparing themselves for possible loss. Mothers of very pre-term babies (under thirty four weeks) have told me how they consciously tried to block off all feelings for their tiny children because of a terrifying fear that they would lose them. There is generally great pain associated with this because for most it is an impossible, if unnatural task. Nonetheless, the complicated feelings connected with the unconscious protection from attachment will have enormous implications for the future relationship of mother and baby and the child's development.

The mother might feel inadequate and unable for the task ahead. Linda's mother certainly did. When her delicate, tiny baby returned home, she was afraid to handle and therefore care for it and handed Linda over to a maternity nurse, who acted as surrogate mother. Raphael-Leff states that 'a mother of a Pre-term baby may feel guilty and wonder what she has done, or what she didn't do to enable the pregnancy to proceed to its normal conclusion'.[6] If she has been through a difficult birth, the mother may not feel maternal and any bonding is made difficult if the baby is incubated, which will mean mother and baby will be separated, maybe for a number of weeks.

The difficulties are amplified if the baby is transferred to a neonatal intensive care unit where it will be very hard for the mother to get close to her baby. Frightened to get too attached to her child and protecting herself from possible loss, the mother of a pre-term baby may therefore find it difficult to bond with her infant. Feeling alienated by the machinery surrounding her baby which may be keeping it alive, she may find it hard not to feel that the baby belongs to the hospital rather than to herself. She may feel useless and a failure, since it seems that machines and medical treatment, rather than her love and care, is keeping her baby alive.

Several studies have indicated a significant relationship between postnatal depression and complications at delivery.[7] This is hardly surprising. It is particularly so when the mother has had a general anaesthetic and is often unable to care for her baby for the first few hours after birth, or if the baby is away in a special care unit. Immediate mother/baby contact is very important to the bonding experience and if this contact is not present, then it is inevitable that both the mother and her baby will suffer. The baby, lying alone in a cot which will appear strange and cold, will cry and want the comfort of its mother. And the mother, who may be sore and bruised or dazed with anaesthesia, will feel her breasts fill with milk and will want her baby. A mourning process begins to happen, as the mother grieves for her baby, as well as for the hoped for experience which has been denied her.

The caesarean mother generally takes longer to physically recover than a mother who has had a natural birth, because she has had an 'operation' which requires considerable medical after care. This means that, in addition to the psychological effects already mentioned, she has to cope with a weakened physical condition and recovery from a procedure which has been a shock to her system. Just as the mother bears a physical scar which will heal with time, it must be acknowledged that she may carry an emotional scar, which may take far longer to heal.

Given the magnitude of the experience, the way it is handled by the birth attendants becomes vitally important. Some women choose to have their babies at home, because they feel they can be more in control of their own birthing. Many women fear that the interventions of medical personnel will interfere with their instinctive ability to give birth. They are afraid that they will be set off course and lose control of their own bodies in labour and ultimately that the sanctity of the experience will be denied them. Given that labouring women are in a state of extreme vulnerability, they will be especially sensitive to the tone of voice and physical ministrations of their carers, remembering for a long time afterwards what the midwife or the doctor said during the birth and their attitudes during the labour and delivery. This means that the birth attendants must be very careful not to violate the sensitivities of the labouring woman. Respect for the sanctity of the experience would ensure that this is possible.

Observations on a more general scale about the effects of different types of birth experience do not, however, do justice to the intricacies of the actual labour and birth process. Many things will influence the way an individual woman will labour and give birth. Much will depend not simply on the way a woman has prepared for her baby's birth, but also the subtle dynamics at work on the particular day or night, such as the place and time of labour and the emotional climate and attitudes of those attending her. It is worth taking a closer look at the process of actually giving birth and in particular the experience of labour. Let us step into the labour room and look more closely at the experience and through some of the birth stories that follow, let us examine more closely the psychological factors that influence a labouring woman and the actual experience of giving birth.

In the Labour Room

Where Inner and Outer Meet

Labour and birth represent a time when the inner and the outer meet. These words can be a wonderful description of the meeting of mother and baby for the first time after many months of 'knowing' each other inside; it can also describe the emergence of the baby from a state of becoming into that of being; or it can describe the interaction of the inner forces operating in the labouring mother with those in the environment. All these things take place at that time and I have used the phrase 'where inner and outer meet' deliberately, as an attempt to describe in some way the delicate and yet powerful nature of the birth process, where what happens outside as well as inside is of prime importance and to describe the intricate interrelationship of the environment and the labouring woman. I am talking about something which is very difficult to define, but has to do with the subtle connection between all people and things, between our thoughts and our actions and the influence we have on each other.

Few Boundaries

An aspect of my work as birth teacher is to attend the labour and births of my clients, at their request. Over the years, I have attended many different types of births. I have consistently found that the labouring woman's emotional and mental state, *as well as that of those around her*, will affect the progress and outcome of her labour. This point is very important, given that it is in the nature of the experience that there are few boundaries between the labouring woman and her attendants and it is therefore incumbent upon those who attend her labour to suppress or contain negative thoughts, feelings, judgements or prejudices which may influence her in any way. A frightened or suspicious midwife or an impatient obstetrician will create a frightened, stressed or frustrated woman in labour.

I have been with many women in labour and have been able to observe the exquisite sensitivity of the birth process to environmental as well as interior factors. I have seen women labour relaxedly in the safe surroundings of their home, only to find that on arrival in hospital their contractions stop and labour appears to cease. Is it not conceivable that this may have something to do with being disturbed while in labour, with having to get into a car and sit uncomfortably for some time, leaving their familiar and safe environment to arrive somewhere strange and having to succumb to the ministrations of strangers?

Studies of animal and human behaviour show that disturbing the process of birth has a negative effect on the progress of labour. Animals will normally seek out a private and secluded place in which to give birth. Women, too, need to feel safe in order to surrender to the sexual and primitive force of birth. The 'nesting instinct' often referred to in the hours or days before a woman goes into labour is a natural phenomenon designed to prepare a woman for her imminent labour. It often takes the form of needing to organise or clean one's house, as though getting the place ready for the birth. I woke up one morning in advanced pregnancy and decided that this was the day I was going to spring clean the entire house! Possessed of amazing energy, I set to the task. Luckily, at that time we lived in a small apartment so the cleaning did not take too long! That night, I went into labour, about two weeks before the expected date.

Many women will find that they have a need to prepare their 'nest' or home, or if they are giving birth in hospital, their room (which is not always easy), so that it is conducive to giving birth in. Some modern hospital maternity units are aware of the need for women to feel 'at home' in the labour room and allow her to take a radio or cassette player with her, together with any objects which may be important to her. Dr Michel Odent, obstetrician and author of many books on birth, designed his maternity unit in Pithiviers, France, so that the rooms were simple and bare of furniture, save a low platform or bed and generally painted in dark, restful colours, as opposed to the clinical white glare of the modern hospital room. He found that labouring women are drawn not only to dark spaces, but also to water and so birthing pools have become an integral part of some maternity units now. If conditions are not right, the labouring woman may be unable to proceed, because she does not feel safe enough to do so.

I have witnessed women's labours pause, and in some cases stop, in what appears to be a physiological 'clamming up' reaction when someone who is less than sensitive to what is happening enters the room. I believe that one person, the wrong person or the right person, can change the course of an entire labour! This is understandable considering the openness and vulnerability of the woman in labour. Safety and protection is a basic human need, particularly during an experience like giving birth.

Giving Birth

If the environment is negative, if fear abounds and defensive medical practice is allowed to thrive, such as breaking the waters to detect any signs of distress in the baby during a perfectly normal labour, this is likely to have a negative effect on the mother. Time and time again I have found this to be true. Similarly, if the mother is herself fearful and defensive, this will affect how she will be in labour. Fear prevents love and inhibits growth. It can stop labours and make birth difficult.

One of the most interesting observations I have made in the course of my work is a significant pause in labour, when a certain point has been reached. The most obvious one is at the onset of the second stage, when the labouring woman is declared to be fully dilated and ready to give birth. Sometimes there appears to be a natural lull in the process, maybe to allow the expectant mother to gather her strength in order to begin the work of pushing out her baby. To those in attendance, it may seem as though there is nothing happening and the labour has stopped, whereas the woman is simply enjoying a lull in her contractions. Unfortunately, exhortations to push by those who are keen to deliver the baby usually serve to put the woman on the defensive and it is not unusual for a great deal of time to elapse with the threat of forceps before the delivery is complete. This is an example of what can go wrong during a birth if the attendants are not in tune with the mother, who may feel she is being forced to give birth. Sometimes the birth can take some time and we must learn to wait for the process to unfold in its own time. I have long felt that clocks should be banned in labour wards.

All creative processes contain lulls. It is part of the natural order of things that creativity is cyclical. There are times for things to happen and there are times for things to be. I am reminded of these words by T.S. Eliot in *The Hollow Men*:

> 'Between the idea
> And the reality
> Between the motion
> And the act
> Falls the shadow

Songs From The Womb

> Between the conception
> And the creation
> Between the emotion
> And the response
> Falls the shadow
>
> Between the desire
> And the spasm
> Between the potency
> And the existence
> Between the essence
> And the descent
> Falls the shadow.'

Sometimes the baby's head may be visible, but the mother refuses to push. I have often wondered if this is an expression of fear, but I believe it to be an inhibitory reaction, a defensive closing up which is due to a variety of things, but in first mothers is commonly a fear of letting go. A labouring woman needs to feel safe in order to let go; indeed, all humans have the same basic need for security in the face of instinctual processes. The urges of the second stage of labour involve a particular kind of releasing to the rhythms and propulsions of one's body and is very similar to sexual surrender. Most of us would not make love in a room full of people!

On the other side of things, I have seen women in labour whose progress is slow, suddenly dilate two or more centimetres when a particular person leaves the room, or conversely, when another person comes into the room! All this points to the influence of other people and the environment on the progress of a woman's labour. Further than this, it points to the fundamental interconnectedness of all things, where everything has an influence on everything else. It points particularly to the importance of holding oneself in awe before the sacred mystery of birth. It points to the need to respect the individual birth process of every woman.

Giving Birth

Positive Mother: Wise Woman

It is interesting to note that the French word for midwife is *sage-femme,* which translates as wise woman. Giving birth is a rite of passage. It is a soul experience and therefore potentially transformative. As with all initiatory experiences, in childbirth there is a need for a guide, a wise woman, a helper or facilitator, who, by virtue of being initiated herself, will assist the pregnant woman's passage into motherhood and new life.

I have found this need to be given expression in the pregnant woman's desire to find a positive mother figure. Often this will be projected onto birth attendants, antenatal teachers and midwives. This means that the emotional bond between the expectant mother and the person whom she chooses to help her give birth will be important and must be honoured. Obviously this will be a particularly strong urge or need in women whose inner mother is wounded, such as those who have had a negative or difficult mothering experience and those who are themselves the daughters of wounded mothers. This will usually mean that there are emotional difficulties or complexities about giving birth and about mothering in general and it may mean in some cases that the pregnant mother's relationship with her own mother is problematic. There are many varieties of wounded mother and each projects onto her birth experience what she most needs to heal in herself. You will see this illustrated in the following birth story.

Susan

Susan was a woman of twenty-nine when she came to my classes to prepare for the birth of her second child. Her first child, John, had been born some three years earlier and the experience had been very distressing. Susan had had a very medicalised birth which had resulted in John being delivered by forceps. By the time she came to me, Susan was very bitter about her experience. She was ambivalent about her new pregnancy and riddled with fear that the first experience would be repeated. She told me that she had experienced John's birth as not only painful and traumatic, but profoundly disempowering in that she had felt controlled and abused during her labour. She had experienced many of the medical staff as intrusive and unhelpful, forcing her through a labour and birth over which she felt she had no control.

Understandably, after such a difficult start, she had had subsequent problems bonding with her child. Her feelings about the birth had affected her relationship with her son and her husband and it was not difficult to see Susan's desperate need for a better birth experience that would help heal her last one. Not surprisingly, Susan carried a mother wound and though I had no actual knowledge of the nature of her relationship with her own mother, except that it was a problematic and emotionally distant one, I knew it must have a part to play in her birth story. I knew also that Susan was unhappy and at times even depressed and that for her, the next birth experience carried hopes of healing old wounds. The wounded mother in Susan, since John's birth, had all been projected onto the hospital, the medical staff and indeed the obstetric system.

Susan's emotional state was expressed in her tense and unyielding body, which made it difficult for her to adopt some of the yoga positions in class. This was curiously at odds with her naturally strong, lean and supple figure. I felt that Susan's natural grace could have made her a dancer, but that somehow this potential lay hidden beneath a somewhat wooden exterior. It was like seeing something plain and lifeless, but sensing a deeper beauty trapped inside. Susan was the clearest example of how emotional states are taken into the body and expressed through what Reich called 'body armouring.' Reich was a therapist who wrote much on the influence of thoughts and feelings on the body.

Susan's anger, pain and hostility, were all held in her body. She was extremely hostile to hospitals and wanted to have her next baby at home. She tried to obtain a home birth, but without success. With my help she settled for a domino delivery. This meant that she would be delivered in hospital by a group of midwives she knew and who would have cared for her during her pregnancy. And she would return home some six hours after the birth to be cared for by the same midwives, thereby assuring continuity of care. Although this was not what she really wanted, the domino system was an acceptable compromise.

Through regular classes and contact with me and the other women in the group, Susan softened a little and began to open up to the possibility of a new experience. It was beautiful to watch this gradual unfolding in her body which slowly reverted to its natural suppleness, so that she could now accomplish with ease the yoga postures and stretches that hitherto had been difficult for her. Her physical abilities were accompanied by a gradual serenity and peace of mind. Susan became more beautiful as she softened into her pregnancy and the approaching birth.

As time and her pregnancy moved on, she asked me if I would be present at the birth. She needed me, she said, to help her give birth in the way she wanted. As it happened, Susan was three weeks overdue and I had already left on my summer break. Seeing this might be a possibility, I had asked her to meet with me before I left, so that we could part without her feeling abandoned and alone. This we did and I think it made a big difference to how Susan was to experience the birth of Jessica. Jessica came into the world quickly and without complications, with Susan describing the experience as wonderful and fulfilling.

I believe that there were many things which helped Susan have a good birth experience. One of these was the emotional bond which evolved between us during her pregnancy. There is no doubt that I became the wise woman, or the positive mother figure that Susan needed to help her transform her past birth experience and to open her heart to a new child and a more positive birth. In fact, Susan had gained so much in self-confidence that she was able to do it without my being there. In other words, our work together had been done, she no longer needed me as she carried inside her at that time, enough of a sense of herself as good mother to give birth to her baby in the way she wished. In psychological terms, Susan had internalised, through the transference, a positive and supportive mother image.

Susan was a wounded mother who was in danger of carrying her wound with her into her new pregnancy and birth experience and who therefore desperately needed a positive mother to facilitate her new passage into motherhood. In my experience, transferences (or emotional attachments), both in the therapeutic environment and outside of it, are accentuated during pregnancy and childbirth. This is because childbirth is an archetypal and potentially transformative experience and many pregnant and postnatal women will form deep emotional attachments to their midwives and birth teachers.

Susan's story reflects the importance of finding a positive mother in order to begin to heal a negative mother wound. Of course the mother wound can be very deep and go back many generations and layers of experience. For example, a woman may carry her mother's wound, who carried her own mother's and so on. Again, it is a natural thing to seek healing and pregnant women are no exception. If we are wounded in a particular way, then we often need the help of others, or another, to cross the bridge to freedom.

The Wounded Mother in the Birth Room

Each woman's 'inner mother' has a profound influence on her labour and birthing experience. Many women are unconsciously influenced by their negative mother image, as it is during pregnancy and childbirth that the negative mother is most commonly activated. A mother wound will gape during this time. For some women, it will be as though a finger has been placed in the wound, though it may be the first time they are even aware of having a wound.

There are many reasons for this. The extra physical and emotional demands of pregnancy and childbirth, together with the vulnerability, instability and psychic openness of the pregnant woman mean that her capacity to contain is stretched, like her body, to its limits and sometimes beyond it. Women need to be emotionally and physically strong to feel comfortable in pregnancy and childbirth. If a pregnant woman carries a negative mother image, then she may find it hard to adapt to the special demands of pregnancy and motherhood and at some level will not feel right. This means that, particularly for those women who have not experienced their own mothers, as nourishing their needs as children, the task of giving birth and caring for a new baby may be difficult. Not having had a positive mother role model will make it harder for the new mother to adapt to the enormous changes that motherhood brings.

I would like to present another birth story which illustrates a wounded mother reaction and confronts the problem of containment. Throughout pregnancy and during birth, the problem of containment is ever present, both physically and psychically. There is so much going on at both a physical and psychological level, that it is often hard for the pregnant woman to deal with it all herself. One way of handling this is through projection. The psychological dynamics of projection in pregnancy is the same as at any other time. Looked at through the eyes of the mother, this means that the doctor, midwife, birth teacher, partner or friend, will become so important to her that she fears she will not be able to cope with the experience of giving birth without them.

More subtly, in the case of the wounded mother, it may mean that her hopes of a good birth experience lie entirely with the person onto whom she has projected the positive mother. As we have seen, the experience of pregnancy and childbirth can appear overwhelming to some women who are afraid they will not be able to deal with, or contain, all the thoughts and feelings that come up during pregnancy. Such was the case with Celia, who needed to express her fears in a safe place (in therapy), before she could unfreeze and begin to face her impending labour and delivery.

Another way of dealing with aspects of pregnancy and childbirth which are felt to be potentially overwhelming is to try and control the experience. This is what happened in Karen's case.

Containing the Uncontainable

Karen

Karen's story illustrates a particular mother wound and a difficulty with containment in pregnancy. I met Karen when she was only two months pregnant. She was of eastern European descent, in her mid-twenties, tall and very beautiful. Her exotic good looks, however, were marred by a hard, sour look. She rarely smiled. Karen was referred to me by a midwife colleague with the words, 'She's very difficult. Try and talk some sense into her', meaning that I was to try and get her to have her baby in hospital, something which of course, I was not prepared to do. Karen was pregnant with her first baby and wanted to have it at home. She insisted that nothing would persuade her to have her baby in hospital, where she felt that she would end up having to have drugs. Though she had no previous experience of childbirth, she knew that she wanted to have the baby naturally, with little or no medical intervention.

Karen was always arguing, fighting the system, fighting the midwives, even fighting her husband, whom she felt was unaware of what she was going through. Once I got to know him, I found this to be true, in that he was not supportive of her needs, though he agreed to go along with her decision to have their baby at home. In the course of our work together, both with Karen alone and jointly with her husband, I became aware of the difficulties of the task before us. Although Edward was outwardly agreeable to whatever Karen wished, he clearly felt unable to participate.

I had no actual knowledge of Karen's relationship to her own mother, except what she told me briefly. She lived abroad and they did not see each other very often. Karen had never got on with her mother and had left home as a rebellious teenager. From other things she told me, it seemed she had been in conflict with various authority figures since growing up. She had hated school and refusing to go to college, got a job as an au pair and then various modelling jobs.

Giving Birth

She was an exceptionally beautiful woman, but in a rather magazine front cover sort of way. There was a certain hardness about her which struck me as unmaternal. I would even have said there was something masculine about Karen. Her rebelliousness and hardness were curiously at odds with the softness and beauty of her obviously pregnant body. In the antenatal classes, I discovered how rigid her body was. Although she was determined to prepare herself for the task of giving birth and so practised yoga weekly in order to loosen up, she was in fact very physically unyielding and even stiff.

Observing Karen, I was reminded of what Carl Jung writes about the negative mother complex in his 'Psychological aspects of the mother archetype.' He writes of the mother complex in the daughter leading to the exaggeration of maternal instincts or the rejection of them. In a section entitled 'Resistance to the Mother', he suggests that this kind of daughter knows what she does *not* want, but is unsure as to what she *does* want. She is resistant to the power of the mother in all its forms. This means that instinctual processes such as childbirth will be a problem. Karen was rebelling against her own mother; she was resisting and fighting herself as potential mother and she was at odds with the maternal institution as represented by the hospitals and the midwives.

It was clear that Karen wanted and needed support in her search for a home birth, something not easily achieved in the area where she lived. I helped her in her quest, while working weekly with her in the antenatal groups, trying to help her loosen and strengthen her body. As her pregnancy progressed, there was a certain 'softening', but as the day of the birth approached I became more and more apprehensive. I had a sense that Karen was somehow actually blocking her potential experience of the positive natural birth she so consciously desired. She was so determined to have no pain relief, no medical intervention, no hospitalisation, that it became obvious that this fight to control her birth experience was masking a deep fear of the experience itself. Karen had asked me to be present at the birth, but only *if* she had to go to hospital.

Songs From The Womb

The following is an account of the birth of her daughter who was born two weeks late. Karen was three days in labour. She laboured all through the day and night and into the next day at home, attended by two midwives, who finally decided to transfer her to hospital. She was not progressing in labour. Furthermore they said, the 'presenting part' (of the baby) was 'badly applied.' This is a term used when the baby is not pushing down enough on the neck of the womb during contractions, thereby slowing down the labour. It also meant that Karen's cervix was very slow to dilate to allow the baby through. It was as if her body was refusing to open up.

I got a call early in the morning. Karen had been in labour for nearly twenty-four hours and was to be transferred to hospital. She wanted me there and I arranged to meet her and Edward at the hospital. When I arrived, Karen was in a terrible state, confused and tired from a day and a night of pain and no sleep. Though she looked exhausted, she greeted me with relief written all over her face.

'Tell them I'm all right. I don't want any drugs, please!'

It appeared from the fetal monitoring that her baby was fine and that her labour, although slow, was progressing without any 'abnormality' or need for medical intervention. As I entered the labour room, she was desperately trying to fight off a well meaning midwife who wanted to administer Pethidine, a strong pain-killing drug. She did eventually take the drug and it enabled her to rest a little and relax between contractions.

Being there and sensing the conflict inside her, I felt my heart go out to her. Doctors came and went and again and again, Karen felt compelled to fight them off, until I took over and began to speak for her. I asked for the consultant, who duly came and after checking that things were fine, he agreed to leave her alone. Because Karen had been in labour for such a long time, the doctors and midwives, anticipating distress in her baby, had wanted to intervene to speed things up, but the consultant confirmed this was not necessary and it would have made things a lot worse.

I could see that Karen's fighting spirit was holding her

back, although I understood her. Karen's deep fear of inter-ference at a time of intense vulnerability, made it very hard for her to let go of the control she felt she needed in order to keep people away. Yet her need for support, at a time when she herself needed to surrender to the instinctive rhythms of her body, created a difficult paradox in her labour. I realise now that in some subtle way, by confronting the medical attendants myself, I became her fighting self, warding off their negative influence and freeing Karen to submit to the rhythms of her labour.

Seeing her so alone, I instinctively found myself between contractions rocking her in my arms, as she, exhausted, lay her head on my shoulders. During the tenderness of these moments, it seemed that she relaxed enough to allow her labour to continue, albeit very slowly. Intuitively, I sensed that she felt herself without any support, except for what little I could offer her and that she found it hard to let go, for if she did, who would be there for her, who would nurture her and who would speak for her?

The situation had been aggravated by Edward's refusal to support Karen in her determination to avoid medical interfer-ence in her labour. Rather than taking up his place as protector of his labouring wife, he became one of those she had to keep away from her. Offering no moral or emotional support, he kept saying that he did not understand why she wanted to go through so much pain. He could not handle her expressions of labour pain and, forgetting the preparation they had undergone together and Karen's determination to avoid drugs and medical intervention, he had withdrawn into a sulky presence which did nothing to help Karen. Tired with the strain of sleeplessness, Edward became bad-tempered and rude in the labour room. Karen, herself exhausted and irritable after a day and night of labour, eventually screamed to me to 'Please take Ed out!'

We went for a walk around the hospital block, which enabled him to vent his rage and smoke a couple of cigarettes. When we returned, he had calmed down enough to be unob-trusive, though he still could not emotionally support his wife.

When we re-entered the labour room less than half an hour later, Karen had dilated two centimetres!

She continued to progress slowly and late in the afternoon I left the labour room for a short time telling her that when I returned she would be ready to deliver the baby. Usually I would have been reluctant to leave anyone in advanced labour, but somehow this felt right. I came back one and a half hours later and found Karen to be fully dilated and the baby ready to be born. With Edward and I supporting her, she pushed her little girl out after almost thirty-six hours of labour. During the delivery of her daughter, Karen tore badly. Again, it was as if she were *reluctantly* giving birth.

In thinking about the experience afterwards, I believe that in so far as I took on some of her fighting, rebellious self, by confronting the doctors and medical attendants during her labour, Karen was able to let go sufficiently to have her baby by natural means. I think it possible that my presence in the labour room and her transference to me (however slight) enabled her to let go to the extent that she did not need forceps and managed to give birth to her baby herself. I mean only that my presence was important to Karen, as indeed any positive mother presence would have been at that time. Regrettably, it is often difficult for women to encounter a supportive mother presence during labour unless they have birth attendants whom they have chosen themselves. Given the nature of modern medicalised childbirth practice, a positive mother presence during labour and birth is not something every woman can count on.

Karen's story is an illustration of how a mother's emotional state can affect the progress of her labour and sometimes even determine its outcome. Karen was in conflict not only with the 'outer' mother as personified by the system, but also with her 'inner' mother. She was overly identified with her masculine, fighting side and resistant to the dictates of her body. I believe she had a deep fear of her own vulnerability and the instinctive process itself and her defence against this was her need to control the experience. We often have a desire to control experiences which expose our vulnerability. Fearful of the feelings, we clam up against life, especially if it means laying ourselves open to painful feelings.

Her difficult labour was further compounded by the presence of her unsupportive husband and the negative atmosphere in which she found herself giving birth. Karen's story also illustrates how the wounded mother is part of the inside story of many women and contributes in its own way to the many difficulties encountered by women in childbirth.

Birth is an experience of existential proportions. Each time a woman gives birth, she faces the possibility of her own death, both metaphorically and physically. There are very few life experiences in which one is so physically and emotionally open and therefore vulnerable. It is an experience which involves not only the labouring woman, but also her partner and attendants in a way which is immediate and imperative, everyone is 'in' the experience and caught up in something which is greater than them. I believe that the 'falling apart' of the body, the disintegration of body boundaries involved in giving birth, leads to fears of a psychic disintegration, which in turn leads to desperate attempts to contain it. By this I mean that the very depth and nature of the experience often creates an instinctive need for protection.

The primitive and instinctive nature of birth is potentially very arousing to those in attendance. The birth attendants will attempt to contain an experience which is potentially overwhelming by using drugs and medical procedures, which are as much used in the defence of their own anxiety as to help the mother. The mother's capacity to contain the experience herself will depend upon her history and her inside story. Usually mothers who have themselves had a positive and containing mothering experience will have a greater capacity to cope with their childbirth experience, including the possibility of a trauma.

Let us move on now from the experience of the mother to that of her baby. In doing so, it must be remembered that in some respects they are the same thing. Mother and baby are inextricably linked, not merely during pregnancy, but throughout the entire birth process. And the way a mother experiences her labour will in its own way leave a mark on her baby. In this way, giving birth becomes also being born, since the technicalities of the type of labour and delivery begin to shape the new mother and the emerging child.

Notes

1.   J. Raphael-Leff *Psychological Processes of Childbearing,* p. 299.
2.   ibid.
3.   ibid., p. 60.
4.   ibid., p. 303.
5.   R.E. Helfer in Klaus M. et al., *Maternal Attachment and Mothering Disorders,* (sponsored by Johnson and Johnson, London: 1974).
6.   J. Raphael-Leff, p. 446.
7.   B. Pitt (1986) *Atypical depression following childbirth.* British Jrn. Psychiatry 11.1325–35; K. Dalton(1971) *Retrospective study into postnatal depression.* ibid 118 689-92.; Jacobsen L., Kaj, L; Nielssen, A.(1965) *Postnatal mental disorders in an unselected sample; frequency and predisposing factors.* British Jrn. Psychiatry 1 1640–43.

Chapter Six

Being Born

In previous chapters we looked at the birth experience from the mother's point of view. We saw how the pregnant woman's inner world interacts with her physical state and we looked at the interrelationship of physiological and psychological elements during birth. We saw how these in turn interrelate with other factors, such as each woman's family history and relationships. We have also considered childbirth in a social and spiritual context, by including how myths and cultural influences inform our psyches and predispose us to behave in certain ways. Through looking in, as it were, at the pregnant psyche, we have explored the experience of giving birth from the inside.

But what of the baby? How does the baby experience being born? Since babies cannot speak to us and since although we have all been born, the birth experience remains for most of us hidden in the deepest recesses of our psyches, we have difficulty receiving an answer to our questions. Most of what we know about the effects of the birth experience on the baby comes from the findings of psychoanalysis, primal and regression therapy and pre-and perinatal psychology.

Interest in the psychological effects of the birth experience has been around for a long time. We are all familiar with the concept of birth trauma and there is a substantial amount of psychological literature from Freud to the present which bears witness to the influence of the birth experience on the development of personality. What has been less examined, however, has been the influence of the mother's thoughts and feelings on her unborn baby's life and the interrelationship of maternal and fetal influences on the birth itself. Only relatively recently has material emerged which reveals the nature of fetal life and the womb experience. There appears to be no doubt that the mother's unconscious processes, as well as her physical state, have a direct influence on her unborn child. Studies have suggested that everything that happens in the womb is recorded at some level in the child's unconscious and further that, without a discriminating ego to act as filter, the fetus takes the mother's feelings and even mental states as though they were its own. In other words, the unborn baby, lacking the sense of being separate from its mother and its uterine environment, absorbs its mother's thoughts and feelings and is deeply influenced by them. Studies have also revealed the fetus and unborn baby to be a much more intelligent and aware being than had previously been thought, capable of learning, memorising, dreaming and even socialising.

The fact that the unborn baby is intimately affected by its mother's emotional state during pregnancy should come as no surprise. Though surrounded and protected by the bag of waters, the unborn child lies within its mother's body. The umbilical cord provides an actual physical channel through which passes not simply nutrients and waste products, but also feelings and thoughts. The unborn child is totally dependant on its mother both physically and emotionally and will absorb and may even react to its environment. I have heard people in a therapeutic context say that they 'felt loved' in the womb. They felt held and nurtured. Others have remembered conflicting or ambivalent feelings, maybe being loved and resented at the same time.

A chronically anxious pregnant mother can contribute to a state of anxiety in the prenatal child who may be born anxious. Continual and persistent unhappiness in the pregnant mother will permeate her womb, so that it may be a sad place for the baby to inhabit. Similarly, if a mother does not consider herself loved during her pregnancy, it may be hard for her baby to feel loved or secure in love. And feeling loved and secure is so vital to life. This does not mean that pregnant women must avoid life, protecting themselves from the normal range of emotions we all go through. Emotional and physical highs and lows are part of existence and will not be harmful to the unborn baby.

Equally, feelings of love and contentment in the mother will have a beneficial effect on her unborn child. Studies have demonstrated that an enriching prenatal environment where the mother may sing, talk to, or even think lovingly about her unborn child, enhances that child's development. If the mother is surrounded by love and support herself, then she will be more likely to feel happy. But chronic maternal stress during pregnancy will be transmitted to the fetus through hormone-induced chemical and physical changes. This happens because maternal hormones, both positive and negative, are released to the fetus through the placenta and umbilical cord.

Labour

How the mother labours will obviously affect her baby. The fact that the mother and her baby are intimately connected emotionally as well as physically, means that labour is a joint process. One of the most important observations I have made as a result of attending different births, is that babies vary widely in their reactions to the stress of labour and birth. Although this statement seems obvious when one considers the effects of different types of births – for example, 'natural' births are less stressful to the baby than drug-induced or medicalised birth – it seems that this is not the whole story. It does not always follow that a difficult birth with medical intervention produces stress in the baby during labour, although this is common; nor does it follow that if a woman has an easy, natural birth, the baby produces no signs of distress. Although the physical health and condition of the mother during labour and the manner in which the birth takes place have a great bearing on the condition of the newborn, it seems that there may be other factors which influence the way a baby experiences being born. Perhaps prenatal life and also constitutional factors are a part of this.

One of the ways of picking up anxiety in the unborn baby during its mother's labour is by observing the colour of the waters. If the waters are clear, all is well. Alternatively, they may be stained with green or brown, indicating that the baby has moved its bowels. This moving of the bowels is a stress reaction, since babies do not normally do this until after birth. Observing meconium stained waters usually puts medical attendants on the alert for potential problems. Since this way of detecting possible stress in the unborn is only possible if the mother's waters have broken, the usual way of assessing the baby's condition during labour is through fetal monitoring, by means of a machine which monitors the baby's reactions to the contractions of the uterus. Normally babies react to maternal contractions by a temporary dropping of their heartbeat and fetal monitors pick up any abnormality in the recovery rate of the heartbeat after contractions. A certain degree of 'dipping' is normal, but there is concern if the baby's heart rate consistently fails to recover or becomes low or irregular. If this happens, the baby is thought to be in distress.

Some women appear to have a normal labour, but their babies show signs of being distressed at one time or another during that labour. Other women with difficult labours can have babies who appear unaffected. It appears that some babies are stronger than others in withstanding the rigours of labour and birth. And what has happened in the previous nine months of pregnancy also influences the mother's labour and her baby's experience of birth.

Birth: An Initiation into Life

Being born is an initiation. This means that it is an experience of powerful proportions which will be vital in its initial impact on the emerging child. Given the nature of birth, it is hard to imagine that anybody might imagine that being born is not a formative experience. Giving birth and being born is, in the natural order of things, a joint effort of both mother and baby. In ideal circumstances, where things are allowed to proceed according to nature, it is an enhancing experience, fulfilling for the mother and formative for the baby. The rhythm and sequence of physical birth is entirely natural and should be allowed to flow for this reason.

What does it feel like to be born? As the uterus contracts, the baby is propelled forwards, the space around it disappears as it is squeezed tightly between the uterine walls, causing the baby's head to be pushed against the cervix. The contractions gradually build up in force and what begins as a stroking squeeze becomes like being caught in a vice-like grip (the force of the uterine muscle contracting is enormous, as was witnessed by a young midwife during a caesarean section). The baby is propelled again and again against the cervix, which must appear like an unyielding wall. Eventually, if all goes well, the wall yields, as the cervix dilates to allow room for the baby to move down into the narrow passage of the birth canal, which it then has to negotiate in order to be born. This will include the natural rotation of his head in order to allow the shoulders to pass through the pelvis. Finally, the baby moves down and out into the world.[1]

The propelling contractions experienced by the baby can be seen as a biological necessity, 'stroking' the skin and helping to stimulate many of the body's systems, particularly the urinary, gastrointestinal and the respiratory.[2] The final major contractions around the baby's chest help squeeze the birth fluid out, which means that the baby can start breathing, and begin its life outside its mother's body, an independent new being. Though the baby is now physically independent of its mother, emotionally of course, the child is not.

Psychologically, natural birth is an ego-enhancing experience. It is an *initiation*. Birth is a struggle that the baby must overcome in order to survive. At a fundamental psychological level, the baby's ability to survive the intensity and strain of the birth experience means a successful initiation, which teaches it about its ability to struggle and survive in the face of life's difficulties. For example, if the birth has been normal and the baby is born by its own and its mother's efforts, an internalised feeling of success in the face of struggle may result. It might also mean that emotional and psychological separation from its mother is facilitated in some way, for if the child is born in this way, then a natural physical separation has occurred. But if a child has to be torn or extracted from its mother, then perhaps emotional separation is made more difficult, for it is as though the birth took place reluctantly. In a natural birth, the model established is of natural separation in its own time.

Modern Birth: Modern Initiations

Our modern way of birth though, has created different patterns. Though ideally it is better to avoid the use of drugs, technology and unnecessary medical intervention in labour and birth, the reality is that in our modern world, it may be hard for us to avoid all or even some of these. Nonetheless, we must try and look at what being born is like in our modern birth rooms where technology has largely replaced nature. The facts are not heartening and explain why an increasing number of women, seeking an alternative approach, want to give birth to their babies outside mainstream hospitals. Modern birth practice is highly dependent on drugs and machinery and women in labour are frequently given anaesthetics of varying kinds. The drug passes through the placenta, providing a dose many times stronger to the baby, so that neither the mother nor the baby can react normally to facilitate the birth. Not only the mother, but the baby is drugged, its respiratory system is weakened and its ability to deal with contractions impaired.[3] Moreover, after the administration of drugs, the mother's contractions are often diminished; worse, they are inefficient because they are out of synch and fail to propel the baby forward smoothly. The use of drugs generally has the effect of disturbing the natural rhythms of labour and birth.

I have observed in women whose labours have been drug-induced, or who have been given drugs in labour, a change in the nature of the contractions. With a practised eye, it is very easy to see the difference between the contractions of natural labour and those of a labour where drugs are present. The natural rhythm of birth is broken. Janov contends that for the baby, a drug induced labour must feel 'like going through a compacting machine, the uterus acting rather like a compacting chamber, its movements strong enough to crush, but not rhythmical or forceful enough to propel the baby smoothly down and out into the world'[4]. With the influence of drugs, the baby's body is in an unnatural position and anaesthetised, it cannot move to aid its own birth. And although no-one knows exactly what the baby's involvement is in its own birthing, drugs will not help the child to struggle out of its mother's body and into independent life. We know that most unborn babies in the last few weeks of pregnancy begin to physically prepare for birth by placing themselves in the right position in the womb, face down with heads flexed and chins tucked in.

Not surprisingly, fetal distress tends to be greater in labours where drugs are present, particularly where they have been used to start or augment labour. The induced contractions are unco-ordinated, a-rhythmical and less efficient. Women find them more painful than natural contractions and therefore difficult to handle without recourse to painkillers. The natural rhythms of labour are less intense and easier to cope with, because of the smoothness of the process, where each contraction is followed by a break. Another result of using drugs in labour is that antidotes may have to be given to the newborn. This usually means an injection to counteract the numbing effects of the anaesthesia already absorbed by the baby, which may be inhibiting its ability to start breathing. Although we live in an age where drugs and anaesthesia have become part of life, an evaluation of their deficits as well as their merits becomes increasingly important at a time when drug-induced illness is on the rise. One of the most serious implications of using drugs in labour is that studies are emerging which link drug addiction in adults to the use of drugs at birth.[5]

Sometimes a birth will be assisted by forceps. Even in a labour which has progressed normally and without the use of drugs, there may be a natural lull in contractions at the onset of the second stage and just before delivery of the baby, when it may appear that the mother's propulsions will not be sufficient to birth her baby. And because we may find it hard to wait for nature to take its course, panic pushes many doctors into completing the birth by using forceps. Or, more rarely in natural labours, there may be an obstruction to natural delivery. This could be due to various factors from the position of the descending baby, to physical or emotional blocks in the labouring mother. Obviously most women will want to avoid forceps and in my experience, sometimes the threat of forceps is enough to push a mother into giving birth spontaneously! Or it may have the opposite effect of inhibiting her even further so that whatever is blocking the birth is doubled.

When I was giving birth to my daughter something of this nature happened. I was slow in second stage labour and the midwife was getting concerned as the baby failed to arrive. Exhausted and disheartened myself, I overheard her and the doctor discussing forceps, something which I knew I wanted to avoid absolutely. When the doctor went out of the room to give instructions for the forceps to be sterilised (I was giving birth at home), I gathered all my strength and pushed the baby out, just in time. I am thankful that I was giving birth at home, for I know that if this had happened in hospital, then it would have been impossible for me to avoid the use of forceps.

Delivery by forceps is more common, however, following very medicalised labours when the mother has been anaesthetised as in, for example, an epidural or spinal block. When the drugged baby is about to be born, the doctor often has to use forceps to complete the delivery, because the mother cannot feel the sensations in her body to push out her baby. Janov suggests that 'the pulling involved in forceps delivery is often too strong and from an improper angle, so that the baby cannot properly rotate and is scraped along the sacral bone, often emerging with large bruises along its face and head from the harsh metal forceps'. It must be remembered that in the natural course of being born, a baby will rotate so that its shoulders can fit through its mother's pelvic outlet. This is much like what happens to the handlebars of a bike when you try and manoeuvre it out through a narrow doorway. This natural movement of the baby's head during normal delivery is very beautiful to watch. I have been very fortunate to observe this on video. The film is called *Birth in the squatting position* and featured women giving birth in South America with no medical intervention whatsoever. It is an extremely moving experience to observe nature at work and to see the natural and implicit order of birth. These babies needed no help in being born. There is no way that metal instruments can mimic this movement of birth. In extreme circumstances of course, they do what they can, but there is no doubt that most women, given a choice, should avoid forceps.

Obviously this is not an easy journey for the baby, but it is not over yet. How is the newborn received once it has finally emerged from the womb? Once it is born, it may be carelessly handled, blinded by harsh lights, the umbilical cord cut too soon so that the baby is deprived of its full quota of oxygenated blood. Cutting the cord too soon would feel to us as though our air supply had suddenly been cut off. Or the baby may be isolated from human contact and placed in an incubator or cot for a number of hours. It may be subjected to painful and invasive medical procedures, such as incubation, before finally being put down and left alone, wrapped up in sheet which feels rough to the baby whose skin is sensitive. Additionally, the baby's frequent need for medical attention following a very medicalised birth will mean that it will be separated from its mother for those first few crucial minutes after birth. This means that there will be an interruption of the natural bonding process, for all animals greet their young straight after birth.

Frederick Leboyer, French obstetrician and author of *Birth Without Violence*, was particularly concerned with the way a newborn is handled and advocates gentle birthing procedures, such as bathing the newborn in warm water immediately after birth and delaying the cutting of the cord until it has stopped pulsating. Aware of the formative nature of the birth experience and the sensitivity of the newborn, his methods are designed to make birth easier and gentler. Although with Leboyer's influence, health professionals are increasingly aware of the sensitivity of the newborn to the harsh stimuli of life outside the womb, gentle births are usually still at the insistence of the mother/parents.

This should concern us, for studies have begun to emerge which suggest a relationship between forceps deliveries and a later predisposition to violent behaviour.[6] Researches into this area continue, which mean that the impact of birth procedures on the emerging child cannot now be denied or minimalised.

Birth by Caesarean

The percentage of babies born by caesarean section is alarmingly high in most western countries. There are a variety of reasons for this, though it is fair to say that the nature of our modern medical system has created many of them. Being born by caesarean section has certain implications for the baby's psychological development and for the mother/baby relationship. Caesarean birth creates its own particular myths and with many more people being born this way than years ago, it becomes increasingly important to listen to the voices of those who have come into the world via a different route.

One such person is Jane English whose explorations into the meaning of her own caesarean birth gave rise to *Different Doorway: Adventures of a Caesarean Born*. This book explores some of the psychological and social implications of being born caesarean. English points out that people born by caesarean operation come into the world in a different manner to the majority of the population and that this in itself creates a need to look at the psychological and social consequences of caesarean birth. Since we are all affected by our prenatal lives and the way we have been born, it could be, for example, that caesarean born people relate differently.

Being Born

Early psychological literature on caesarian birth has tended to view it as an abnormality and so the negative psychological aspects of the experience were highlighted. English writes from a transpersonal perspective, making the point that while at the level of soul intentions there is no such thing as an imperfect birth, at the level of personality, of everyday life, there may be.[7] I find this a helpful way of seeing things, for it means that whilst we can acknowledge the difficulties that a particular experience creates in the life of the individual, we can appreciate its lessons.

And there is certainly no doubt that the experience of caesarian birth is very different to normal vaginal birth.

What might be the psychological implications of caesarean birth? Let us look first at the physical differences. We know that the contractions of labour prepare a baby for its birth by stimulating its nervous system. The intensity and force of second stage contractions prepare the baby for life outside the womb through stimulation and therefore activation of vital organs. Without that experience, there may be inadequate activation which can be a factor in the child's developmental process. Another problem specific to caesarean birth is that of blood supply. In a caesarean section, the baby is lifted up above its blood supply (as opposed to a vaginal birth where the umbilical cord is in a lateral position in relation to the baby), the cord is perpendicular and it is inevitable that some of the blood travels backwards to the placenta.[8] This means that for that time, the baby is being asphyxiated.

Then there is the question of timing. Owing to the suddenness of birth by caesarean, it is common for many of these babies to be confused and some particularly anaesthetised ones are dozy and lethargic. This makes the baby unresponsive and contributes to the difficulties the mother may have in bonding with her child. The natural timing and instinctive harmony of birth is upset. A caesarean birth takes very little time as compared to normal birth. In later life, this situation can result in difficulties with inner timing. Adults born by caesarean commonly report a feeling of impatience in the face of process and a desire to get things over and done with in as short a time as possible. Many say they cannot rest until the task they are currently undertaking is completed. The sense of it being a natural thing to stop and take a break before resuming and completing a task, for caesarean born people is often difficult to grasp and accept. Of course, one could say that we are all influenced by the timing of our births and the caesarean born is distinguished only by the short length and the intense quality of time involved in its own particular case.

Caesarean birth involves being anaesthetised, either by local or general anaesthetic. Regression therapy has found that this aspect alone can be extremely distressing. Reports indicate that the baby, acutely aware and sensitive to its environment, is affected by everything that happens during its birth. Quite apart from the confusing effects of the anaesthesia on the baby, it appears that babies react to their mother's anaesthesia. This often involves a terrifying feeling of being alone in the face of birth's tumultuous upheaval. The child may have a sense of a dead or powerless mother who cannot help her baby into life. The baby is alone, caught up in a terrifying and even life-threatening experience. Not having its mother 'present' at the birth can profoundly affect the baby at a deep level. The baby may feel abandoned and depressed, lost and confused.

I have also noted that it seems a particular characteristic of those adults born by caesarean to experience, in analysis or therapy, a feeling of being stuck. This in itself is common to many, but with these clients, there is the added dimension of waiting to be rescued by the therapist. There seems to be a kind of helplessness right at the moment of psychological birth, when the client has done the work and is on the threshold of moving forwards into a new level of conscious awareness. The psychic baby has great difficulty in actually being born. I have wondered whether this is partly an unconscious defensive reaction for the caesarean baby does not push to be born, but is born by being pulled out by the obstetrician. The pattern thus formed is of becoming open by being intruded upon. A defensive reaction is normal in the circumstances.

108

Being Born

Life Struggle

Some of what has been said about the mother's psychological experience of giving birth by caesarean will also apply to her baby. A child born by caesarean section, particularly non-labour caesarean is, in similar fashion, deprived of its birth struggle. The infant is suddenly removed from its mother and has no time to prepare for life outside the womb. One minute it is in the womb, the next it is out in the world. Non-labour caesarean babies, unlike their labour siblings, have no sense of struggle, or of a birth *process*. They are simply suddenly 'pulled out.' They are denied the struggle to be born. This does not of course mean that they have not had their own particular struggle in the womb, but if we are to consider birth as the initiation that it undoubtedly is, theirs is different.

We know that many traditional cultures and spiritual customs include a symbolic birth as part of their initiation rituals. These rituals usually take the form of a struggle through the forces of darkness and danger and an emergence into the light and a new life. Nature herself provides us with numerous births, as even a flower has to struggle and push upwards through the soil, using a tremendous life force to break through the dark earth, to flower and blossom in the sunlight.

'The force that through the green fuse drives the flower
Drives my green age; . . .' *(Dylan Thomas)*

A caesarean baby is denied in part, or in whole this initiation by struggle and so may be born with an enormous frustration, as this life force, this emotional and physical energy remains unexpressed. I believe that the struggle to come into life is a vital aspect of the birth process.

'The force that drives the water through the rocks
Drives my red blood; . . .'

Since birth is archetypal, I believe that the baby lives its life in the womb *expecting* and preparing to be born. What happens if this need to struggle into life is unexpressed? One possible answer is that it is carried by the baby into postnatal life and given expression in later behaviour and perhaps ways of relating to others.

The baby thus born enters a world for which in some senses it is ill-equipped. The difficulties of its task of beginning life outside the womb may be increased, as it has little or no experience of a successful struggle. Not having fought and emerged through the birth canal, the caesarean baby lacks the coherence, the structure and the definition that this experience brings. In simple physical terms, the mother's birth canal provides the boundaries or walls that the baby needs to push against in order to be born to independent life. Without this experience, it may be difficult for the caesarean baby to form a sense of self, since the first physical contact it has is with the gloved hands of the obstetrician who extracts it from the womb.

Separation

Thomas Vernay has shown us that caesarean babies crave physical touch in postnatal life. This has been found to be directly linked to the baby's lack of experience of the intense sensory stimulation of birth through the birth canal. This may be expressed later in various ways. There may be a craving for physical intimacy and yet a fear of it. A sense of lacking adequate physical and psychological boundaries is particularly common. This could be described as not feeling that one has adequate skin or protection from the outside world and others, or that one is particularly prone to taking on the problems of others. The positive side to the caesarean's sense of limitless boundaries is a natural ability to sense and connect with spiritual reality. I imagine this has to do with the very real fact that the caesarian child's journey from womb life into birth is shorter. On a soul level again, the transition from spirit to incarnation and biological birth is different. The sense of living still in a spirit state of all pervasive perfection may be still resonating in the infant's body.

Whilst this ability may facilitate the individual's spirituality, it is usually not acknowledged until later in life, when the person has become more whole and clearer about personal boundaries. This extra sensitivity is often linked to difficulties in sensing and feeling oneself to be a separate entity. So although we crave for what we have not had, say, physical and emotional intimacy, lacking a strong sense of self, we are at the same time afraid of losing oneself in the other person.

What makes us realise that we are separate from one another? The point at which we begin life outside the womb must give us a first basis for a sense of self. And surely at its most primitive, the struggle to emerge from inside the body of another gives us a sense of being separate. Not achieving physical separation in this way at birth must affect our sense of being separate or 'other', and our ability to emotionally separate later on. Those who have studied the behaviour and relationship patterns in adults born by caesarean contend that this difficulty with separating arises as a direct result of their caesarean birth experience. The ability, or lack of ability to separate emotionally, is something which becomes highlighted in deep psychological work with all individuals and it seems entirely appropriate to include the circumstances of birth, since the nature of the physical experience of caesarean birth has much to teach us about the dynamics of psychological separation.

Though it must be remembered that none of these ideas about the caesarian born person's experience are absolutes, developmentally, the caesarean baby's initiation into life will differ from that of a baby born vaginally. The confusing, numbing effects of anaesthesia and drugs, combined with its own and its mother's condition which may necessitate separation, mean that bonding with the mother is not something the baby can count on. Removed from its mother's body and denied the *struggle* to be born, the baby may emerge without a sense of containment, without possessing boundaries and without an adequate basis to form a sense of self. In a way, you could say that the caesarian baby's struggle happens after birth.

Because we are human, it is possible that some mothers whose babies were born by caesarian or indeed any medicalised birth may feel guilty about what they feel their child has been through. But we should remember not only the great resilience of the human soul to adversity, but also that conscious aware-ness is all. Many mothers of caesarian babies have spoken to me about this and have asked what can be done to mitigate what appear to be the negative effects of such a birth. My answer is always that if the mother is aware then she can help her child transform its experience of birth. It means for example, that she will know that her child's need to push her boundaries by say being difficult, may be as a result of its not having done so at birth. And remembering that every cloud has a silver lining, meaning every adversity has its gifts.

The Premature Baby

If a baby is born prematurely and, as is often the case, by cae-sarean section, the difficulties are compounded. A premature baby is 'not ready' and depending on the degree of prematu-rity, generally is ill-equipped to deal with life outside the womb. If the baby is severely premature (six weeks or more), its first contact outside its mother will be the gloved hands of the obstetrician, the masked faces of the birth attendants and tubes and machines. Its first few days, weeks and even months may be spent in an incubator. The baby may bond with a machine and later may feel isolated, alone and that a glass wall separates them from other people. Added to this, if the baby has survived a life-threatening medical complication (for example, placental haemorrhage), its system may be slow to recover from the shock of the emergency operation and the trauma of its birth. Deprived of the normal struggle to be born, too small to fight and ill-equipped to deal with life outside its mother's body, the baby's immature organs pushing and being forced to do what they are not ready to, the premature baby may give up and may have to be kept alive by machines. The child may emerge from this early experience later on, confused as to whether it was being kept alive for itself or for others, that is, in the service of the medical need to save lives.

Being Born

Linda's birth story expresses much of the anguish of premature and caesarean birth.

Born Too Soon: Linda's Story

Linda came to consult me because she was training as a psychotherapist and she needed to undergo a training analysis. I liked her immediately. She was a lovely woman of thirty-three years, married with three small children. She had huge, dark eyes in a face that seemed too small to hold them. Her eyes were strikingly beautiful, but they radiated a hunger which felt somehow unconnected with this world. It was as though they held thoughts and memories of a time as yet unknown. They were deeply spiritual eyes.

When I first saw Linda, I imagined her to be much younger than she was, for there was something very immature about her. And yet, paradoxically, she appeared very precocious. I often had the urge to tell her that she was far too young to worry about such adult responsibilities as running a home and minding children. And yet at times she appeared old and very wise. She was capable of quite amazing insights, both about herself and others.

This strange mixture of childishness combined with wisdom is something which, I later discovered, is connected with the unmothered child. The wise child is often the unmothered or abandoned child, who has to develop precociously in order to survive. These children, who may not necessarily be orphans but who are emotionally deprived, neglected or abused in some way at a very young age, develop a special ability to cope with their lives. They are profoundly sensitive to their environment and to other people, developing antennae so that they can quickly sense what is expected of them. They are so frightened of offending others, especially those in authority, that they are always trying to find ways of pleasing, particularly if they think they will be loved. So the unmothered child often has special gifts, like acute sensitivity and intuition, which enable him or her to sense things well before others.

Linda often seemed to voice what I was feeling, before even I knew it myself. She would surprise me with acute insights and yet I often had the urge to hold her in my arms and rock her, like a baby, for in our work together, she often became very sad and very little. At those times it was as though she was shrinking before my eyes. When, during sessions, we reached and touched those areas in her life that hurt her, almost at once, it felt as though we were propelled way back, to a time she did not know, but could still feel. She felt the loneliness and pain of being a tiny baby and of being alone, without her mother.

Linda had been delivered two months prematurely by caesarean section. She was born of a depressed, exhausted and ill mother who already had two children. Linda, who had been gravely ill at her birth remained in an incubator for six weeks and it was a further five weeks before she was taken home. This meant that Linda was already nearly three months old when she came home to her family. Her mother, still depressed and physically bruised by the birth and feeling herself to be incapable of mothering such a delicate baby, left the care of her child to a maternity nurse hired for that purpose. Linda told me that the need for 'special care' so early in her young life had made her feel isolated from the rest of her family. Her start in life, apart from her mother, father and siblings, made bonding difficult. Deep down, Linda felt that she was different. She had started life in an institution, not unlike children who are orphaned or adopted.

In therapy, Linda re-experienced the profound sense of despair and the raw emptiness of the unmothered child born prematurely from her mother and left alone to survive. Because her birth was so traumatic, it was often difficult for her to cope with the pain of what came to the surface during therapy. She found it hard to experience me as caring of her. She felt I was not really there for her. It was only a job for me and besides she was paying me. Though I knew that I loved her, I also knew that she could not feel this love and that she would not be able to feel it for some time. Knowing that she had a deep need for love and at the same time knowing that she was as yet too hurt

114

to feel it when it was there, was one of the most painful experiences of my life as a therapist.

Linda, beneath her efficient and capable veneer, was very fearful. She feared most especially being alone, for at those times, she told me, 'I am afraid of the emptiness, of finding no one and nothing. Then I begin to panic.' Her fear expressed itself as a pervasive terror. The terror of aloneness, when the tiny baby cries out and there is no answer; there is only an emptiness. I believe Linda at those times was remembering and feeling what it was like to be in the incubator. And if the premature baby is so tiny that it needs medical attention, as Linda did, then it may be a struggle to stay alive. The tiny baby emerges into life but, unlike its healthier peers, it cannot relax and start to thrive in its new environment. Instead, every moment is fraught with anxiety as the newborn baby struggles to simply stay alive.

As an adult, Linda had difficulty allowing herself to thrive and grow and her life often mirrored the intensity of her original birth struggle, meaning it had a particular all-or-nothing quality. There is living and there is dying, but there is nothing in between. Each breath is taken as though it may be the last; there is no certainty that there will be another one. Even in adult life, possessed of a loving family of her own and secure financially, Linda found it hard to relax. She always had to be doing something; simply being was impossible.

This all-or-nothing quality is something which mirrors the physical experience of caesarean birth. In normal delivery, the baby experiences the ebb and flow of the contractions during labour, the coming and going, the natural wave of contractions. Non-labour caesareans do not experience the natural rhythms of labour and one of the psychological effects of caesarean birth seems to be that the person will tend to relate to people and things with an intensity which has that uncompromising quality. This could also be described as a black and white attitude to life. Again, this is not written in stone and represents a general tendency which indeed may be present in some people not born caesarian.

During a particularly deep regression, Linda re-experienced the terrifying conflict between breathing (taking in life) and feeding (taking in nourishment). As a tiny premature baby, she could not do both at the same time. Her system was too immature to cope with both breathing and sucking, so that every feed left her choking and gasping for air, her whole body revolting against the 'torture', yet powerless to do anything to stop it. This very early experience developed in Linda a subtle yet pervasive conflict with nourishment in all its forms. Though not overtly suffering from an eating disorder, Linda would be unable to eat when deeply emotionally upset. In affective terms, Linda's birth and early experience made it difficult for her to form emotionally satisfying relationships. In her adult life she chose partners who were unresponsive and emotionally distant or cold, thereby recreating her early deprivation. She described her life with her husband as an emotional wasteland: a poignant description of her first life experience. When things were particularly difficult in her relationships, when she felt unloved and insecure, then she had great difficulty swallowing food. Feeling constantly sick, she generally lost weight every time she underwent an emotional crisis.

Psychotherapeutic work with Linda revealed her to have developed the compliant self of the child who wishes to please and continually waits to see what is expected of her, never developing a healthy creative self. It was hard for Linda to simply be herself and to assert her needs, for deep down, she did not really know who she was. When compliancy takes the place of creativity in the emotional life of an individual, it means that there is a loss of soul. This meant that Linda could not play and could not simply *be*. It meant she could not relax, for at rock bottom there was always an anxiety about life.

Thomas Vernay has found that many prematurely born adults tend to feel rushed all the time; he suspects that the feeling that they will never ever catch up is a direct result of their prematurity. They begin life in a hurry and many years later, they still feel that way. Prematurely born adults often feel vulnerable, small and insignificant; it is reasonable to suggest that this is partly related to their prematurity. This is certainly something thing I could relate to and something which I found was a common mon trait in both friends and clients who were born premature. My sense of being small, vulnerable and insignificant used to irritate a partner of mine who saw me as strong and powerful. This same man who was acutely intuitive, understood that my occasional bouts of minor illness were my way of saying, 'I'm very delicate, look after me!'

I have observed in adults born by caesarean section, an unspecific yet pervasive anxiety, which at its most extreme, is sometimes experienced as panic. Such people report a sense that something terrible is about to happen, often in relation to journeys. Linda was always particularly anxious when she was about to go on a journey. She also worried about me when she knew I was going on holidays abroad, as this often would involve a plane trip, which was particularly bad. Linda hated flying and suffered from a mild form of claustrophobia. Claustrophobia is far from uncommon in adults who were in danger in the womb, either from a threatened miscarriage or, as in Linda's case, from her mother's haemorrhages in late pregnancy. At one stage during the course of her therapy, Linda was unable to travel in tube trains (the underground), or to go into lifts. She would panic at the thought that she could not get out. She felt shut in and dangerously confined. At that time we used such things as natural remedies and meditation tapes to help her deal with her fear. However, as we worked through successive layers of her psyche, this improved.

Many caesarean born people have a fear of knives, operations and hospitals and feel very powerless, stuck and unable to get out of whatever particular situation they happen to be in. There is often the sense of being trapped in something and lacking the capability to break free. Of course the sense of being trapped in a relationship, a job, or a particular life situation is not something exclusive to caesarean born people, but the inability to see one's way out, or to feel that one has a choice in the matter, is very reminiscent of the physical experience of a caesarean birth, where the baby is born not by its own efforts or that of its mother, but by the intervention of surgery. Also, the nature of the operation, where a mother's body is cut open and the child removed, gives rise to gruesome and primitive fantasies about human sacrifice. Though these fantasies and images lurk in the darkest recesses of our psyches, they may be kindled by the birth experience. It is not surprising that many caesarean born people feel very uncomfortable in hospital surroundings. Linda told me that the latent smell of disinfectant and anaesthetics in hospitals made her sick and frightened.

I believe that no one is left unmarked by their birth experience and how it happens is crucial to that person's development. Certain patterns are laid down at the birth which later become blueprints for future behaviour. In the following chapters we will look at the psychological implications of what has been said about the experience of giving birth and being born. This means that we must turn our attention from the experience itself to making sense of it. We must look more closely at ways of healing the wounded mother and the emerging child. Perhaps this may begin by recognising that birth is a soul experience, which like all soul experiences has a transformative potential. It is only by recognising and acknowledging that birth is a profound metaphor for change that we can harness its healing power and begin again to heal the wounds of birth that have become so apparent in our society and in our individual hearts.

Notes

1.   Janov. see above; especially pp. 33-47.
2.   ibid., p. 35.
3.   ibid.
4.   ibid.
5.   Jacobson. B., Nyberg.K. et al. (1988) *Obstetric pain medication and eventual adult amphetamine addiction in offspring.* Acta Obstetrica et Gynecologica Scandinavica 67; 677–82. Jacobson B. et al. (1990) *Opiate addiction in adult offspring through possible imprinting after obstetric treatment.* British Medical Jrn. 301.1067–1070.

6. A. Raine et al. (1994) *Birth Complications combined with early Maternal Rejection at age 1 year Predispose to Violent Crime at age 18 years.* Arch. Gn. Psychiatry vol. 51.

7   J. English (1993) *Being born caesarean: Physical, psychosocial and metaphysical aspects.* Pre-and Perinatal Psychology Jrn. vol. 7 (3).

8. Janov, p. 3.

Part Two

Healing The Wounds Of Birth

Chapter Seven
The Lost Feminine

*There is a void felt these days by women and men who suspect
that their feminine nature, like Persephone, has gone to hell.
Wherever there is such a void, such a gap or wound agape, healing must be sought in the blood of the wound itself.*
                         Nor Hall, *The Moon and the Virgin.*

I believe that the problems women encounter when giving birth
today as a result of the denaturalisation of childbirth are merely
a reflection of a general and wider problem, that of the lost feminine. The feminine is a creative archetypal force that lives in all
men and women. It is not gender related. The repression of the
feminine in this sense refers not merely to the subjugation of
women, but to the considerable devaluation of instinct, feeling
and intuition, all that is natural in us our soul values.

Jungian psychology has deplored the repression of the feminine in our modern society. Carl Jung spoke of the loss to the
world of the will of nature and described many of our contemporary problems as loss of soul, which were as a result of
modern man's alienation from God and nature. He saw that our
modern world has suffered greatly from the divorce of spirit
from matter and mind from body. Not only is the wounded
mother a personal or individual thing, it is also collective. And

122

just as individuals have suffered a mother wound, so has the modern world. Healing our personal wounds is always possible, but at some level, this will not be enough. It will not be enough for society to change birth practice. Healing the collective mother wound means reinstating the feminine in our culture so that childbirth is perceived and managed differently. This means reinstating the neglected mother archetype.

Our Inheritance

An understanding of the concept of archetypes and how they influence our lives is useful in that it helps us understand the profound nature of certain life experiences like birth, marriage and death. One of Jung's main discoveries and contributions to psychology has been that of the 'collective unconscious' which can be described as an immense pool of information about human culture and history which is available to us in the deeper part of our psyches. The collective unconscious is made up of universal human experiences that have evolved over time and contains psychic possibilities or primordial images which pre-dispose us to approach life in certain ways.

These psychic patterns, which are called archetypes, are inherited. Each infant is born and begins life carrying intact the contours of its own life possibilities. The environment therefore does not grant personality, but brings out what is already there.

These are the rudimentary images which govern behaviour and could also be described as inherited modes of functioning.

Outer Behaviour

Archetypes can be defined as the inherited part of the psyche and are evident only through their manifestations. They can be recognised in outer behaviours, particularly those associated with such universal experiences as birth, marriage, separation and death. Archetypal patterns possess a numinous energy which exercises a strong influence on our lives. Jung described it thus:

'Archetypes are psychic forces that demand to be taken seriously and they have a strange way of making sure of their effect. Always they were the bringers of protection and salvation and their violation has as its consequence the perils of the soul known to us from the psychology of the primitives. Moreover, they are the infallible causes of neurotic and even psychotic disorders, behaving exactly like neglected and maltreated organs or organic functional systems.'[1]

It is difficult to describe archetypes, except to say that they are forces which are fundamental to human existence. Experience fleshes out the innate blueprint which can then be observed in outer behaviour. They influence us in many ways. They inform our thinking, feeling and behaviour so that for example, when we become pregnant we will be guided to behave in a particular way in relation to carrying a child and ultimately becoming a parent.

Anthony Stevens discusses archetypal expectations in the human psyche and what happens if these expectations are frustrated. Describing archetypes, he suggests that they choreograph the basic patterns we dance to throughout life; indeed it is 'the archetype and not our conscious ego, that pays the fiddler and calls the tune'.

Structures

Archetypes do not only influence human behaviour. They are also the blueprint for the natural order of organic matter. Jung proposed not only that the archetypal structures were fundamental to the existence and survival of all living organisms, but that they were continuous with structures controlling the behaviour of inorganic matter as well. Thus, 'archetypes precondition all existence and are manifest in the spiritual achievement of art, science and religion, as well as the organisation of organic and inorganic matter'.[2]

Thinking of the world from an archetypal perspective enables us to perceive its wholeness. The notion of archetypes binds people and things together. It mends the split between matter and spirit. It restores soul to human life. Others have noted something similar. Jean Liedloff, author of *The Continuum Concept*, contends that modern man, having strayed from the way of life to which evolution had adapted him, is set on a course that can lead only to destruction – of himself and, ultimately, of the entire planet. Applying herself more particularly to the mother and child continuum, she warns us that if we are to survive, we should go back and recover from our ancestors the wisdom we have lost.

Liedloff describes the human continuum as the continuity of experience which holds the echo of expectations and tendencies from their primordial foundation in the human species. Since archetypes form the basis of life through inherited modes of behaviour, we are born with an instinctive expectation of a suitable culture, in which we can develop our tendencies and fulfil our archetypal expectations. As Liedloff states, 'in each life form, the tendency to evolve is not random but favours its own interests'.[3] Our individual continuum, though whole, forms part not only of the family continuum, but also of the community continuum and further, the species continuum, each forming part of the all-embracing continuum of life.

Division Of Nature

As a Jungian, it was not difficult for me to see why our birthing practices have become in many ways alien to us. In a society which has largely banished goddess consciousness from our lives, Demeter the mother goddess had been condemned to a virtual underground existence, only to emerge passive and wounded. The word goddess in this context is really a description of universal feminine energy and Demeter (goddess of agriculture, fertility and marriage in Greek mythology), is a descriptive term for the maternal or mother archetype which is the ultimate source of all creative processes.

In *The Goddess Within*, the authors Jennifer and Roger Woolger, ask the question, 'How is it that Demeter's sacred functions have come to be so demeaned and so neglected in the modern world?'[4] They suggest that in order to answer this question we must look back at the social history of the goddesses during the development of western civilisation. With the advent and rise of patriarchy, the role of the mother goddess became secondary and the functions of childbearing, mothering and agrarian culture were given an inferior status. 'A sharp division arose at that time between the urban gods and goddesses who reflected the values of a rising warrior patriarchy and the more traditionally rural divinities who were all essentially matriarchal and attached to the land.'[5] This meant that urban 'civilised' values were held in higher esteem than more rural, instinctive ones.

Scientific Rationale

The shift in consciousness from matriarchal to patriarchal values had dramatic social and psychological consequences. Women all over the world who had hitherto been the guardians of the sacred mysteries of birth and death and were powerful healers, began to be shunned, persecuted and often even put to death. As the Middle Ages waned and patriarchal medicine emerged, women healers everywhere were driven underground by those who feared their powers. This was the period of witch hunts and burnings and the division of spirit from matter, where 'healing was dehumanised by the belief that all living things could be controlled if they were conceived of as machines'.[6] Jeanne Achterberg, author of *Woman as Healer*, points out that women, caught in the divorce of spirit from nature, were absent at the birth of modern medicine.

This 'separation of mind, body and spirit tore at the very fabric of women's healing power'[7]; such values as compassion and intuition had no place in the scientific rationale of modern medicine. This meant that the mother goddess had been demoted and the feminine values of nurturing and bearing children, healing the sick and tilling the land became secondary to those of power and social position.

Medical Management

The devaluation of the feminine was complete, however, when Demeter sustained her most intimate wound in the denial of her birthrights, something which is reflected today in the medical management and control of childbirth and the general devaluation of the role of the mother in western culture. Today, motherhood is generally considered not so much a blessing in itself but more as time taken out of a demanding and self-enhancing career. I believe that western civilisation is nursing a deep mother wound and that this is but one rarely perceived aspect of the general repression of the feminine which has deeply marked our world. In Jungian terminology, one can say that the mother archetype has been badly wounded. If a society lives by the power of a wounded archetype, this means that an aspect of that archetype is repressed and lives in the shadow. Jung tells us that denial of the archetype and suppression of certain instincts will result in neurotic and even psychotic disorders, for what is repressed returns uninvited usually in a destructive manner.

Repressed Archetype

We are all the inheritors of the wounded mother. The repression of the feminine has meant that we have lost touch with our instincts and worse, that we have become alienated from the natural in us. In the denial of birthrights, however, patriarchy strikes its cruellest blow to the already wounded mother. Wielding the knife of power, patriarchy attacks Demeter at her most intimate and vulnerable and she, divested of her dignity and stripped of her strength, limps into passivity as resigned and broken. She can but suffer the indignities perpetrated upon her at a time when she is least able to resist.

The supremacy of patriarchal values has meant that childbirth, formerly the province of women, where women were tended by women, has fallen into the hands of a patriarchal medical profession intent on controlling rather than facilitating the process of birth. In practice, this has meant the effective death of home birth and the subjugation of midwives, as women are shepherded into centralised units to have their babies. The inheritors of the wounded mother today are those women who, depressed and disillusioned after the birth of their babies, flock to their doctors, therapists or alternative practitioners seeking to be healed from a wound which they often do not know they possess. It was these women who came to my consulting room.

The wounded mother can be seen in our hospitals and nurseries and in our childbirth culture and practice. Pregnant women are often not sustained in their all-important job of giving birth to new life. Instead, their task is often made more difficult by an institutionalised system largely ignorant of their emotional and spiritual needs. As I saw each woman struggle to regain the positive or Nurturing Mother and to heal the mother wound in the months preparing for the birth, I prayed that the system would help and nurture her when the time came for her to give birth. Very often, I saw her robbed of whatever she had gained during the months preparing for birth and I saw her deprived of life-sustaining nourishment. The mother embodied in our modern medical institution of childbirth is often in fact, a negative mother, a Stone Mother. Modern childbirth practice, in its insistent emphasis on the physical and denial of the emotional and spiritual, has failed its children.

The Stone Mother

The mother archetype is supremely important and the source of all life. If she is wounded in her nurturing aspect, it will have serious consequences for the world. Jean Shinoda Bolen, Jungian analyst and author, writes about the mother archetype in many of her books. She describes the four faces of the Great Mother as 'The life-giving, Nurturing Mother and her opposite, the Death Mother; the Ecstatic or Dancing Mother and her opposite, the Stone Mother'.[8] Using the metaphor of the myth of Demeter and Persephone, Bolen explains that when

128

the Nurturing and Dancing Mother is not present, an emotional wasteland results:

'In Greek mythology, Demeter, goddess of the Grain, the most giving and bountiful of the Deities, who represented the Mother Goddess at a time when patriarchal religions were becoming predominant, became the Death Mother when she refused to let anything on earth grow and would have allowed hundreds to die of famine. Her heart and compassion had turned to stone. She had become the Stone Mother.'[9]

The theme of the Stone Mother can be witnessed today. New babies, born all too often to anaesthetised and traumatised mothers themselves disconnected from the Nourishing Mother, are, in effect, being born into a world where the Nurturing Mother is absent. It is very difficult to be nurturing in an environment which is emotionally barren. In a wasteland, the soul withers and the heart freezes. Contemplating the fate of these babies, I thought of the newborn children in the nurseries of the world, who, though fed and changed, were not touched, picked up, or held. Though physically cared for, these infants pined and waned, as though somehow they had lost the will to live. Paediatricians and psychiatrists such as John Bowlby described this condition as resulting from lack of mothering. It was prevalent to institutionalised babies languishing in hospitals, nurseries and orphanages, some of whom actually physically died from emotional neglect. These babies suffered from an obscure disease called 'failure to thrive', which really means collapsing from lack of love.

Babies and children who are not loved die; either they die physically or they die psychologically. Similarly, if a mother is wounded, she may die psychologically. Sick at heart, she will find it hard to become the Dancing Mother. The reality is that many babies today are born to depressed mothers, mothers in whom the archetypal Mother in her positive aspect is missing, women who are wounded and who have consequently become Stone Mothers. They are Stone Mothers because in them, the ability to love and nurture has turned to stone. They are Stone Mothers because they are themselves wounded. And traumatised, they may find it hard to love. Human nature protects itself and so it is a natural reaction to recoil in the face of pain. Whether psychically or physically, many mothers are anaesthetised and therefore out of touch with their instinctive nurturing abilities.

Age Old Expectations

Despite this, most women will want to experience childbirth positively. The lost feminine does not stop women from hoping, wanting and instinctively expecting and preparing for, a good birth experience, one which necessarily involved them as active participants. Wanting to heal the mother wound, many of these women find themselves at odds with a lot of current birth practice and shun the reclining position during labour and delivery, preferring instead freedom of movement and choice of position, usually upright, for delivery of the baby. The supine position reduces the labouring woman to the position of passive patient, rather than of a woman actively giving birth. After all, actively giving birth to their own children is every woman's birthright and something we have been primed to expect from our primordial roots.

Having a baby is a normal biological function. Women have given birth since the beginning of time and a woman's body is designed to carry, give birth to and feed her young. For almost two million years, women have squatted, knelt, stood, crouched or sat, sometimes with the physical support of other women, to have their babies. Many gave birth alone, unaided by anything save their own instincts. They have laboured and given birth not only by the custom of their tribes, but according to the dictates of nature and their instincts. Very rarely did women lie down to have their babies.

The predominance of upright postures for delivery of the baby has been confirmed and noted by anthropologists and historians alike.[10] This is evidenced from artefacts, ancient pottery and statues, all depicting women in various positions for childbirth. Aztec fertility stone figures depict a squatting goddess; a Mayan pottery depicts a goddess kneeling with the baby emerging from between her thighs. A relief from the temple of Kom Ombo in Egypt shows a woman giving birth in the kneeling position and birth in the same position can be seen on a marble figure from Sparta, about 500 BC. Greek and Roman reliefs depict women giving birth on a stool supported by two assistants.[11]

From the beginning of time, women were the guardians of the secrets of birth and death and, as such, were uniquely suited to their role as midwives. The original midwives were more often than not the mothers of the women giving birth and theirs was a singularly intimate and supportive role. Childbirth was essentially a family event of deep social, cultural and spiritual significance and not a medical feat requiring the ministrations of professionals.

Native Wisdom

In a recent book entitled *Birth Traditions and Modern Pregnancy Care*, Jacqueline Vincent Priya examines traditional birthing customs and compares them to modern pregnancy care. What is most striking is the difference in prevailing attitudes to childbirth. She writes that, in traditional cultures, giving birth is the special concern of women, in that women alone control and take responsibility for pre- and postnatal care. It appears that giving birth is always central to these women's lives and intimately connected to their identity as women. And most importantly, an acknowledgement of this is inherent to the system. Birth is a family affair and each member has a part to play in something which is not only part of the natural order of things, but also reaffirms each family member in their own knowledge of nature and life. Traditional societies place birth in a much wider context than the narrow physical approach of the modern medical system, by taking account of the spiritual aspects. Most importantly, traditional societies have preserved birth in its rightful spiritual and social context and therefore fulfils each woman's archetypal expectations.

This is in stark contrast to prevailing ideas about childbirth in the 'developed' world, where not only the social and spiritual aspects of the birth experience remain unacknowledged, but giving birth is considered to be a 'medical problem fraught with all sorts of danger requiring the ministrations of professionally qualified personnel'.[12] Women in traditional societies turn to their mothers and other women for advice and help during their pregnancies and whilst giving birth, so that in this way, the natural archetypal wisdom is passed on from mother to daughter.

Priya points out that because of the medicalisation of childbirth in the west, women have very little of this wisdom to pass on to their daughters. Pregnant women have to rely on books and the medical profession for information, advice and coaching on how to give birth. Alienated from native childbearing wisdom, pregnant women flock to prenatal classes, often run in centralised units such as hospitals and health centres, hoping to learn techniques and procedures to deal with what they are led to believe is a painful medical event which can be managed and controlled by technology and drugs. Generally, very little of what they learn is designed to increase their self-confidence. Rather than being encouraged to connect with their own instinctive knowledge and ability to give birth, they are taught to place their trust in 'professionals.' Instead of being empowered to give birth, any trace of ancient knowledge is taken from them as they are forced to surrender to a system which knows best. Discouraged, these women suffer loss of soul, because the positive aspect of the birth experience is denied them.

Changes

It is only in the last few hundred years that childbirth customs and practices have begun to change. Towards the middle of the seventeenth century, with the advent of forceps, birthing practice began to shift. Madame de Montespan lay down to have her baby so that Louis XIV could watch the birth of his child. Women then began to lie down to give birth and were assisted by male obstetricians rather than midwives. It became the fashion for ladies of the upper classes to give birth in a recumbent position with the male obstetrician in attendance. As forceps gained in popularity, the birth stool, which had been in use since the second century AD, lost favour.

In the middle of the nineteenth century, chloroform began to be used by women in labour. Queen Victoria was responsible for its coming into practice in England. Delivery under anaesthetic, with the woman lying down, became widespread. This birth position lent itself more easily to the convenience of the attendants who performed procedures designed to facilitate their task, rather than to help the woman in labour. And so the birth chair gradually gave way to the delivery tables and beds of the nineteenth and twentieth centuries. Women slowly began to lose touch with their instinctive, natural ability to give birth, succumbing instead to the ministrations of medical attendants who 'performed' the birth for them. Giving birth had now become a medical event rather than a natural process.

Although the 1960s and 1970s saw a resurgence of interest in home births and midwifery and women have since begun to question the role of technology in birthing practice, we are very far away from re-establishing birth as an instinctive process. Our current birth practices reflect the way in which we live. Our babies, so often brought into the world with the use of drugs, forceps and high technology, are born into an unnatural world, a world suspicious of and devoid of the feeling values of positive mother. Many of our babies are born with a violence that is bred of fear, with the consequence that the first sensation a newborn encounters is often pain and the first emotion fear. With our engineered birth practices we have bred or at least contributed to a violent society. Regrettably, it is possible to say that giving birth today has become not a natural and sacred event but a technological feat.

Having strayed from our cultural inheritance, having lost touch with the wisdom of our ancestors, we have become alienated from our own natures. We have become depressed and debilitated. The medicalisation of childbirth, focusing as it does on the physical, means that giving birth and being born has largely been stripped of their spiritual significance. And when we lose touch with soul, much of life loses its meaning.

I believe that the way we birth is the way we live. We need to examine the ways in which we give birth if we want to change society and become healthier human beings. I think that the way to do this is to become more aware of the emotional and spiritual significance of the birth experience. We must begin to heal the wounded mother both in a personal and collective sense.

Notes

1.   C.G. Jung *Collected Works* 9(2) para 266.
2.   cited in A. Stevens *The Two-Million-Year-Old Self* pp.13–14.
3.   J. Liedloff *The Continuum Concept*. (New York: Addison-Wesley, 1977), p. 26.
4.   J. and R. Woolger *The Goddess Within* (London: Rider Books, 1991), p. 304.
5.   ibid.
6.   J. Achterberg *Woman As Healer* (London: Rider Books, 1990), p. 101.
7.   ibid.
8.   J.Shinoda Bolen *Crossing To Avalon* (San Francisco: Harper Collins, 1994), p. 176.
9.   ibid., p. 177. •
10   J. Balaskas *Active Birth* (London: Unwin, 1983), p. 4.
11   ibid., p. 5.
12. J. Vincent Priya *Birth Traditions and Modern Pregnancy Care* Element Books 1992, p. 17.

Chapter Eight
Healing The Wounded Mother

'I feel so useless and so angry at the same time.' Maggie sobs into her tissue, already sodden with tears. She lies in a crumpled heap on the couch, her childlike vulnerability at odds with her ample breasts and body which still hold the legacy of her recent pregnancy. Next to her lies her son Tom, peacefully asleep after his feed. It is her turn to be fed I think, as I watch her struggling to button her blouse. Maggie, though happy with her son, is battling with post-natal depression. At least that is what she has been told she has and Maggie, desperate to talk, has come to me. She wanted someone to help her work through the birth, she said.

'I need to talk about it. I need to tell someone what it was really like. If I don't, then I think that I'll go crazy.'

No woman is left untouched by her experience of giving birth and for some, it will act as a trigger to activate previously unresolved conflicts from the past. Sometimes, the quest for a 'good' birth experience reflects in many women an unconscious need to heal a deep wound in the psyche. This will be particularly poignant in a woman whose own birth was traumatic. On a deep psychological level, the new mother's relationship to herself as mother and to the whole mother archetype will become highlighted as she struggles to adjust to her new responsibilities and status.

Most women approach the birth of their babies with an expectation of having a fulfilling experience and of bonding with their babies. The universal, primal nature of the experience means that most women will want to encounter something special and sacred in giving birth. The spiritual dimension of birth is often forgotten, perhaps because giving birth is such an overt physical experience. And our modern world has suffered greatly from a general divorce of spirituality from nature and mind from body. This has meant that we tend to regard our bodies and all instinctual processes, such as sex and birth, as purely physical and devoid of spirituality or soul. Giving birth and being born are archetypal experiences however, and deeply spiritual and social events.

Unfortunately, the nature of modern medicalised birth has caused many women to feel disempowered and alienated from their own natures. It has led many to suffer loss of soul and to become depressed. These women are wounded mothers. They come to the consulting room after the birth of their children, feeling bruised, angry and very hurt.

Maggie felt this way. The birth of her son by forceps delivery, after a protracted and induced labour, left her exhausted and depressed. She and Tom had been separated for two days. While he was recovering in intensive care from early breathing difficulties, Maggie lay in bed, nursing her wounds and feeling alienated from everyone. What was worse was her terrible sense of guilt that she had found it very difficult to bond with Tom. Separation and the sense that she had failed her baby and herself in having to succumb to medical intervention, made her feel bad about herself. She was not a good enough mother and, even worse, she could not cope. Maggie struggled on, not realising that what she was suffering from was loss. She was in mourning for the experience she had not had, while at the same time battling to come to terms with a birth so unlike that which she had expected.

To make matters worse, Maggie harboured a deep-seated resentment against the medical attendants whom, she felt, had prevented her from giving birth naturally. Uncovering her feelings in therapy would help Maggie regain a sense of herself and also reclaim her birth experience. Putting her in touch with the loss of her fantasy birth would enable her to release the raw emotions that she had previously repressed. The telling of her story and the acknowledgement of her experience by someone who could understand, would facilitate in Maggie a liberation from it. This would free her to bond with her baby and move forward in her new life as mother.

Maggie's story is far from uncommon. Women often need to repeat their accounts of labour and birth again and again. I think this is part of the psyche's way of coming to terms with an experience which has remained undigested because it is too disturbing. In Freud's words: 'A thing which has not been understood inevitably reappears; like an unlaid ghost, it cannot rest until the mystery is solved and the spell broken.'

I have found that it is not only difficult births that need to be replayed, but rather the experience itself, since some mothers regard even a normal birth to be a disturbing experience. For some women, labour and the very act of giving birth can be experienced as a trauma which they need to continually replay in their minds until it can be healed and finally integrated. The replaying is a quest for meaning, for it is only when the experience is understood that it stops hurting.

Potential Change

The pre- and perinatal period is a time of immense change and emotional upheaval. The pregnant and postnatal woman is in a position of potential change, growth and transformation both physically and psychically. With physical changes come psychological changes and the pregnant woman's physical growth and production of a new life can often result in her own psychological growth, particularly if she is in analysis or psychotherapy.

The therapist who works with pregnant women must often contain the fears and fantasies of these women in a way which is special to the situation. Joan Raphael-Leff's psychoanalytic explorations into the psychology of pregnancy and childbirth highlight this extremely well. Pregnancy, Raphael-Leff says, is a state of psychic permeability[1] and great emotional and physical vulnerability, within which many women will feel over-whelmed. In my experience, the greater accessibility of previously unconscious thoughts and feelings can lead pregnant women in therapy to think that they are going mad, or that they may go mad unless they somehow express or release the primitive thoughts, fears and fantasies that plague them. The fear of death and of dying in childbirth, for example, is not uncommon. Bad and all as these fears are, some pregnant women feel that they cannot let go of them without losing their unborn baby[2]. This takes place at such a subtle level that she will not be aware of it. She will only know that she has to contain all sorts of feelings and thoughts that don't usually bother her. This sets up a paradoxical situation, where there is the need to let go and at the same time the need to hold on to something.

Therapy aims to help the wounded person to maximise her own resources and in my view a pregnant woman should be sustained and affirmed by emphasising her positive role as mother, rather than to be opened, dissected and pulled apart. Psychoanalytic work should focus on the containing aspect of therapy. With post-natal women, an interesting extra dimension enters the therapeutic relationship. The therapist has to accommodate the mother/baby relationship as symbolised by the real mother/baby couple, physically present in the consulting room, alongside the mother's own 'inner baby.' The mother's task is to accommodate her baby and since she is so preoccupied with being a mother, it is often difficult for her to acknowledge her own needs. Sometimes the baby and its needs are placed between the mother and her therapist. The opposite is also true: that the mother may feel jealous of what she feels is attention being given to her baby by the therapist, when her own inner baby needs attention.

In the sessions, Maggie recounts her birth story many times, so that gradually, with the telling, it begins to fade from significance until eventually, it takes its rightful place in her psyche.

Rather like an undigested piece of food which must be regurgitated before it can settle, the birth experience will continue to trouble Maggie until it is finally understood and integrated.

'I wanted so much to be there when Tom was born. After these months of carrying him inside me, I wanted to hold him right away and feel we had been through the birth together.' Maggie begins to cry. 'I was so looking forward to it, now it's too late.'

When Maggie said she wanted to 'be there' for her son's birth, I knew she meant that, dulled with anaesthesia and the pain of knowing she had not actively given birth to Tom, she had felt too numb to greet him after his birth. Maggie herself had been born by caesarean section and was separated from her mother for quite some time after her birth. Because of this separation, she had not been breast fed and Maggie felt there had been little or no bonding between herself and her mother. When she had discovered she was pregnant, she was overjoyed. This birth would be different: it would be all the things she had missed at her own birth and, bonding with her own child, she would prevent a repeat of her own early experience. But this longed for experience had eluded Maggie. She couldn't bear it. In the depth and intensity of her despair, I heard and felt the raw pain of the newborn separated from her mother. Feeling unmothered herself, the grown up Maggie had sought to mother her own baby and in doing so to heal her own unmothered 'inner' child.

My work with pregnant and postnatal women involves as it does in any therapy, listening to and bearing witness to their stories. The telling and the listening validates the experience. People all over the world tell each other their stories; groups such as Alcoholics Anonymous survive upon it. Therapy involves the added dimension of interpretation which serves to make sense of these stories, in a way which is meaningful to the wounded person.

In any therapeutic work however, healing cannot begin without an acknowledgement of the depth and nature of the wound. Giving birth and being born are supremely powerful experiences, within which it is possible to encounter the archetype of transformation, or psychological rebirth. The wounds of birth are deep soul wounds, particularly with already wounded mothers. The very nature of soul wounds means that they are often hidden from conscious awareness and may be visible only through symptoms such as depression or physical illness. However, the soul will speak to us in dream images and through our imagination and fantasy life. If we are willing and ready to listen to our deeper selves, then we can begin to heal them. But first we must listen to the stories.

Woundedness

Working with the wounds of childbirth one must acknowledge the transformative power of pain in order to harness the healing potential of the experience. Psychological work of any nature involves the recognition of the possibility for experiences negative or positive to touch us and change us. I find that for many, the experience of pregnancy and childbirth evokes major changes. Sometimes, for example, it is during pregnancy that a woman will first become aware of her woundedness. This might also be the case for her partner and the father of the child. The sight of a defenceless newborn baby will evoke in even the most hardened person, their own vulnerability and dependency. For some, this might be difficult to deal with as it may provoke painful feelings and memories of being alone and abandoned.

At the same time, a newborn baby so innocent and dependent on its parents love, as a tender plant is to the protection of the moist earth and the warmth of the sun, will stir soft, loving feelings in most of us. Nurturing and protecting a newborn baby can help to heal those wounds that are closest to the heart. In therapy, we hear the most painful birth stories, but it is here that the most profound healing takes place, for it is in the nature of things that the most damaging experiences are also the most profoundly transforming.

Sometimes the nature and depth of a soul wound is such that there are often no conscious words to express it. Then dream images will often tell the story. Jackie, for example, knew

140

that giving birth to her son had been a distressing experience, but it was her dream that gave us the details and told us precisely how she had been hurt. Once the story has been told and the person is moved and feels the pain, then healing begins to take place. Transformation starts in the heart of the wound, just as in therapy, it is the wounded healer who heals the wound. The wounded healer is another archetype used by Jung to describe the healing process involved in the patient/doctor relationship. It means that the doctor/therapist, by virtue of their awareness of their own wounds, can activate the healing process in the wounded patient. I knew that I too had experienced a birth wound and that this would enable me to heal others. My awareness of my own woundedness meant I could empathise and share. I could put myself in the shoes of the person I was working with.

The Two Million-Year-Old Within

Carl Jung's work was about healing the soul. He felt that what ails modern man is an alienation from God and nature which he described as 'loss of soul.' When he began his journeys to North and Central Africa and New Mexico, Jung was in search of what he called the two million-year-old within.[3] He was in search of an age old collective wisdom which had been lost or obscured by certain aspects of modern life: 'I unconsciously wanted to find that part of my personality which had become invisible under the influence and the pressure of being European'.[4] These journeys provided Jung with valuable insights into age old patterns of human life and 'confirmed his impression that Europeans had become alienated from their own humanity.' This was because their 'rationalism had been won at the expense of their vitality', and hence their most primitive natures had been 'condemned to a more or less underground existence'.[5] Jung thought that this lies at the bottom of our contemporary anxiety. Man must reconnect with his basic nature; alienation from his nature has led him to lose his soul. This loss of soul has led us to become demoralised and depressed.

Much of our lives in the busy, modern world, with its emphasis on economic power and social position, is taken up with outer tasks which do little to enhance our inner lives. We often forget to attend to the smaller things in life, such as walking in nature, visiting an art gallery, or listening to our dreams and spending time writing our thoughts, or meditating. These are all soul tasks, as letting our imagination flow is life enhancing. Daydreamers at school are usually frowned upon and yet, most if not all creative work involves imagination. Our modern values which honour 'doing' rather than 'being' mean we tend to devalue soul work as idleness or lack of drive. But how many of us, exhausted after a day's work, roll into bed and complain bitterly that we have no time to ourselves? The numinous energy of the soul has been obscured by the relentless anxieties and pressures of modern life.

Jung suggested that in order to regain soul we must pay closer attention to our psyches and to the voice of the collective unconscious in our dreams. Our dreams form the bridge between our inner and outer lives, between our conscious and unconscious attitudes. They have a particular function: to compensate for the one-sided attitudes of the conscious ego by mobilising aspects of the collective unconscious, which can help us. Inside our psyches lies the two million-year-old man. Inside our psyches lies ancient wisdom. Mobilising this wisdom and integrating it into our lives can help heal our souls and restore us to healthy living.

Healing the wounded mother means listening to the lost voice of the soul. What Jung had described as our contemporary illness applies also to childbirth. The two million year-old wisdom, the wisdom of our ancient childbearing grandmothers is cut off from modern childbearing women. Pregnant women, alienated from their own natures, are often alienated from their innate, instinctive ability to give birth. On a profound level, their archetypal expectations had been frustrated and everything that each pregnant woman is primed to expect from her antecedents had failed to happen.

Psychological illness results when the environment fails to

meet the basic archetypal needs of the developing individual. Psychiatrist John Bowlby noted this. He studied the psychological behaviour of very young children who were institutionalised, usually as a result of illness and noted that separation from their mothers had devastating consequences for their future development. The need to attach to a loving parent who is emotionally available on a consistent basis, is a fundamental human need, present in every infant. Those infants and children in hospitals and orphanages for any length of time, suffer gravely, not merely due to separation from their mothers, but also from the unavailability of a consistent carer. Because of the nature of institutions, where different people are involved in the day to day care of the children, a child cannot attach itself to a mother surrogate. And secure attachment in early life helps us form healthy relationships later in life. Lack of this experience tends to make us anxious and insecure.

Stress

Stress is a key factor in most psychiatric illness. The greater the gap between archetypal needs and the environmental fulfilment of those needs, the greater the stress and the more incapacitating the illness. If people are uprooted, like plants, they tend to wither. For many, separation from nature and rural communities leads to a life of stress-related behaviour in large anonymous cities. Jung found that the people who came to consult him were on the whole not severely mentally ill, but rather were suffering from the aimlessness and futility of their lives. He came to regard this malaise as typical of the twentieth century, 'the general neurosis of our age.' He attributed it to the emergence of social institutions that alienated us from our archetypal nature. Incarcerated in large cities, we plant window boxes in tiny concrete spaces to remind us that we are part of nature. Deprived of fresh air and open spaces, our children are confined to play in a few square metres squeezed between tower blocks. As extended families become a thing of the past, we cram everything into one person and then wonder why we suffer from loneliness. It appears that modern values interfere with our perception and recovery of the archetype, which is another way of saying that we have lost our way.

Having strayed from our cultural inheritance, having lost touch with the wisdom of our ancestors, we have become depressed and debilitated. Giving birth and being born have largely been stripped of their spiritual significance. This means that our spiritual alienation is deepened and our soul wounds sink deeper into our psyches. Pregnant women will continue to have dreams of birth and hope and the post-natal mother will continue to have nightmares of maiming and desecration, unless we begin to heal the wounded mother.

Notes

1. J. Raphael-Leff. already cited.
2. ibid., p. 59.
3. A. Stevens *The Two-Million-Year-Old Self* (Texas: A&M University Press, 1993).
4. C.G. Jung *Memories Dreams Reflections* p. 224.
5. ibid., p. 32 in Stevens.

Chapter Nine

Songs From The Womb

*The dream is the small hidden door in the deepest and most inti-
mate sanctum of the soul, which opens into that primeval cosmic
night that was soul long before there was a conscious ego and will
be soul far beyond what a conscious ego could ever reach.*

C.G. Jung *Memories, Dreams, Reflections.*

Linda: 'I have no luggage'

I have found that the therapeutic relationship, along with the
inner and outer forces in a person's life, can activate painful areas
not only of that person's early childhood, but also of his or her
birth and prenatal life. Often themes from the womb will
emerge through dreams and will be especially highlighted during therapy or analysis. Linda, who was born prematurely and
by caesarean section, is an example.

Linda had recurrent dreams of going on a journey, without
her luggage. Dream images are quite specific and it was interesting to see the evolution of the dream during her time in
analysis and the subtle changes in the images each time she
dreamt this dream, which reflected what was happening in her
psyche.

145

In the beginning of her analysis, there was simply no luggage and the dream was accompanied by considerable anxiety about travelling somewhere without having what she needed for the journey. 'I am anxious because I have nothing to wear,' she said. After we had been working for some time, there were variations in the way she set about her journey. At one time, Linda dreamt that she had no luggage, but that this time I gave her a long black dress which was not much but which enabled her to travel. Linda wore the dress and was able to go on her journey with less anxiety than before. The dream image suggested that Linda now had some protection. The dress symbolically represented the *persona*, which is a Jungian term for that part of us which has acquired the social skills to function adequately in the outside world. It was given to her by me and this depicted what Linda had gained at that time in her therapy and through her relationship with me. It meant that she had become a little stronger in herself. Instead of being vulnerable and without the resources to undertake her life journey with security, she had gained a sense of self, however small.

The word persona refers to the actor's mask which was worn in ancient times in ritual plays. Jung uses the term to characterise the drive towards adaptation to external reality and our personas represent the roles we play on the world stage. Sometimes, as in Linda's case, the persona is inadequately formed, often as a result of early emotional deprivation and the person will suffer from lack of poise or social adaptability. Since the persona appears in dreams in the image of clothes, uniforms or masks, someone with an inadequate persona may dream of being at a party naked or badly dressed, or of being on stage and not knowing their lines, for example. Having no luggage, Linda was ill-equipped for her passage. She had no clothes or belongings. She did not have what she needed for her journey into postnatal life. These dreams depicted accurately her own birth which was rushed and premature. At only seven months, Linda was not ready to be born. She had not yet finished growing, both physiologically and psychologically.

During the last two months of womb life, the unborn baby continues to develop in preparation for birth and life outside the womb. To be born before the proper time must feel like being raw, having very little skin or protection. Premature babies are without the extra body fat which is laid down at the end of pregnancy. Psychologically speaking, to be without fat is to be acutely sensitive and very vulnerable. When I met Linda, she was a grown woman with her own children and the tiny vulnerable baby .was hidden beneath many layers of the padding which life's experiences gives us. But her dreams exposed her nakedness, her vulnerability and her need for 'fattening up' so to speak. True love can give us this padding and indeed the unmothered child will do almost anything to find love, but without a well developed discriminating capacity to recognise the difference between conditional and unconditional love, the unmothered child often remains without it. That is, until she begins to find it in herself.

In prenatal terms, the dream image of 'luggage' can symbolise the placenta. The placenta represents that with which the baby comes into the world. Biologically speaking, it is normally delivered after the baby and is examined in detail, since it teaches much to the medical attendant about the uterine environment from which the child has emerged. The function of the placenta in the uterus is to both nourish the baby and remove its waste products. It comes to signify in a particular way the mother. It *takes in* something from the baby (waste products) and discharges or *gives back* to the baby what it needs to survive. After birth, the mother will function in just the same way, for she will read the baby's signals and respond to its needs.

Unborn babies have been observed to play with the placenta and to use it as a pillow during sleep periods. In a way, it can be seen to represent the first object with which the baby has a relationship. Unborn babies having relationships may seem farfetched, but it has been observed. In the absence of a brother or sister, unborn babies use their womb objects, particularly obviously the cord and placenta, to play with.

The baby learns much about the nature of life and its mother through its relationship with the placenta. For example, the unborn learns about its mother's diet, since everything ingested by its mother passes through to it, however filtered. Sometimes there is concern during pregnancy about the ability of the placenta to perform this function of nourishing and removing waste products; in medical terminology, this is called 'placental insufficiency.' The placenta, in many ways, performs the functions of a postnatal mother, in that it sees to the unborn baby's needs. Linda was born too early; she lost her womb environment and placenta (luggage). The dream image suggests that she had no luggage and indeed she did not. But she survived, as do a great many other very premature babies.

How do very tiny babies who should still be in the womb survive outside it? Obviously hospital special care has helped to increase the survival rate of premature babies, so that today babies as young as twenty-four weeks gestational age are surviving. But physical survival is only one aspect of existence. Emotional and spiritual life are an integral part of the human form. And though efforts have been made to humanise hospital care of premature babies, it is doubtful whether a special care unit of a hospital can provide the kind of emotional environment a tiny baby needs.

What does it mean to be catapulted into life before time and without the adequate means to live? Those tiny babies must develop precociously and I think that this must be at some cost to them. Perhaps this could best be described by saying that, for these babies, life is concerned with survival rather than thriving. The very idea of premature birth indicates a type of maternal deprivation of the most primitive kind.

Linda survived her early birth, but it too was at some cost to her. So, healing the wounds of birth means remembering that these are soul wounds that are deeply embedded in the human psyche and in the fibres of the body. They are deep because they are primitive and have no language other than that of dreams and symbols. And since generally we do not become aware of wounds until some time into our adult life, they are old wounds

148

that we have been carrying for a long time. We must treat them and ourselves with the greatest respect and compassion. Knowing that our wounds are also our greatest gifts and acknowledging the transformative power of birth, will help us to have the courage to face them and to begin to heal them.

Katie: 'There Is No One There For Me'

The reader may remember Donald Winnicott, paediatrician and psychoanalyst, whose work I referred to in chapter three. Daniel Stern, developmental psychologist, has also contributed much to what we know of the psychological development of the infant. Both men emphasised the importance of the holding environment and the continual emotional presence of the mother or care giver to the baby's emotional development. Whereas Winnicott stressed the negative effects of environmental factors which might constitute an interruption on the infant's sense of self, Stern was more specific in his elaboration of the same theme. He stressed the importance of the relationship patterns between mother and baby. The mother is needed not simply to care for her baby, but to validate the child. This happens not merely through her love and attention, but also through her presence during important moments of self realisation in the child's life.

Take, for instance, an incident with which most mothers will be familiar; the small child who says, 'Mummy, watch me. I'm going to jump over this puddle. Watch me!' The mother knows that she must watch and that if she does not, or simply glances at her child and does not really take the time to watch and admire, then the experience will have little meaning for the child. This is an example of mirroring, something which is a vital part of human development.

Referring to the mother's ability to sufficiently mirror her child as 'attunement', Stern contends that if there is lack of attunement by the mother to the infant's experiences, such as in the case of a depressed mother, the infant will react by developing a compliant self, as opposed to a true self. The child of a

149

depressed mother will learn very early on that in order to get its mother's attention, it has to act. Soon, the child learns to read its mothers mood and will devise a varied repertoire of attention seeking activities. This means that it can never really relax and just be, for it has to constantly keep its mother in mind. In this case, the mother's own needs, thoughts and pre-occupations will impinge upon her infant's experience and she will not be emotionally available to enter into the baby's own experiences and to share them.

I believe that this same type of experience can happen in the womb, but in a different way. Here the baby is inside the mother and so the seeing and the mirroring happens psychically and internally, in a subtle thinking and feeling way. Though the mother will be aware of her baby, particularly when the child moves in the womb, she cannot see it, so she loves the baby by thinking about it and maybe engaging in such activities as singing and body massage. Mothers often sing lullabies to their unborn babies and indeed some prenatal preparation courses involve group singing. If the father of the baby loves and massages the mother's abdomen and speaks gently to his child, he is already bonding with it. Generally, if the mother feels loved and cared for, she will be happy and this will enhance the unborn baby's womb experience. If, however, she is preoccupied or continually anxious, or involved in activities which will take her attention away from herself, then she is not available to her baby in the same way. This means that for a time, perhaps a crucially long time, the baby is without its mother's attention. Katie was one such child.

'There is no one there for me'. I was to hear these words of Katie's again and again. Katie was a divorced woman in her late forties when she came to me for psychotherapy. Her initial motivation for going into therapy was her own training in counselling. She came from a modest background, but became quite wealthy upon her marriage. Katie had delicate physical health and was often ill as a child. She lost her only sibling, a brother, in an accident. Her brother was younger by five years and by contrast was strong and healthy. He had been very vital and was in the full flush of youth when he died in his early twenties. Katie, newly married and with a young child, was devastated. During the time I was seeing her, her father died and her elderly mother went to live in a home.

When I first met Katie, she was immaculately dressed and arrived for her appointment on time. She was a small, slim, delicate woman with an air of frailty about her. There was an immediate ephemeral sense to our connection. It seemed to me that there was hardly anything there under the elegantly made up and dressed shell. She appeared in a curious way to be 'empty'.

The first few sessions were very difficult, for I found it hard to reach her. I had the constant feeling that I was intruding, that I might easily break that fragile shell and somehow damage her. She told me she was a very private person and found it difficult to talk about herself. Although she had attended a bereavement counsellor for brief periods after her brother's death, Katie appeared reluctant to make a full commitment to the therapy. I quickly perceived this difficulty and explained that I would work with her only on condition that she came to see me twice a week as we had to build up an adequate working relationship. She feared that twice a week would be too much for her. Eventually I agreed to see her once a week on condition that this would be reviewed at a later date.

Katie's early life was that of a sheltered, cosseted and delicate little girl who was often ill from asthma. She spoke of her mother as being a fearful and anxious woman always thinking and voicing the worst. Katie's father was described as a quiet, gentle man who does not appear to have been physically strong, but who had a calm resilience and solidity which Katie came to rely on, saying of her father; 'he was there for me in a way in which my mother was not'. He was protective of his family and the relationship between Katie's parents seemed to reflect his need to control and to be responsible for practically all aspects of their life together, resulting in Katie's mother's dependence on her husband.

Katie's mother had sustained a double loss just before she

had conceived her. Her first baby, a little girl, died at two months of age. Shortly afterwards, her own mother died. This turned out to be extremely significant and was to have a profound effect on Katie.

Katie fell in love with and married her childhood sweetheart John. Within two or three years, having come into an unexpected and sizeable family inheritance, they went to live abroad. But John, who had always been psychologically vulnerable, fell into a pattern of alcoholism and drug addiction. Money and the exigencies of life in the fast lane often exert a price and prey on particular vulnerabilities. Life was fraught with difficulties for Katie who struggled to hold the marriage and help her husband. Their daughter Rosie was born, but Katie became very ill shortly after her birth and was separated from her baby for two or three months while she was being treated in hospital. This made it difficult for her to bond with her baby and exacerbated an already shaky relationship with John. Katie, like her mother before her, had become very dependent on her husband, particularly financially. After years of coming and going, of parting and reconciliation, they finally divorced.

Much of the first stages of the therapy consisted of helping Katie to let go of John. Though they had been divorced for some time, she was very tied to him, not least by the pull of financial wealth which represented security. At some far from conscious level, it felt as though money and power had come to symbolise love to Katie. This made it difficult for her to form a loving relationship for, deep down, she felt herself to be worth nothing inside. Her self esteem was so low that a small dependent part of her would accept any kind of relationship, even if it was emotionally empty or abusive, in return for love. Early emotional deprivation can make us stay in the worst kind of relationships. We stay because we think we can change them. We stay because, blinded by the need for love, we do not pause to see who it is that we have chosen. We stay because we are afraid of being alone.

The only love Katie knew about from John was material in nature. She would say, 'I could break away from him if only I could find someone who could offer me the same things,' (meaning someone wealthy). During the time in which we worked together, she formed relationships with men, often younger than herself, who on the surface appeared to be able to offer her these things. But like many men approaching middle age and still caught in the fire of youth, they were always full of promise, promise which never materialised. Plans were built, but they were for castles in the air. Making a deal and striking it rich was always round the corner. But it all stayed in the never never land of Peter Pan. The part of Katie that was little Princess and Daddy's girl, and who waits to be rescued by her Prince, fitted the Peter Pan in her lover.

But the marriage of Peter Pan and The Princess is doomed to failure, for neither has grown up. These relationships were brief and far from satisfactory for Katie, who, through fear of suffering another love wound, had great difficulty making a commitment in a relationship. Ending the relationship, however, was too difficult for Katie, who had a fear of abandonment and being left alone. She told me she needed to see people constantly and arrange meetings so that she could go out. She could not stand being alone. This paradox between being very dependent on people and being fearful of making a commitment remained with Katie and entered our relationship. She said she didn't want to become dependent on me in case *I would die* and not be there for her. She often seemed to doubt that I could be a reliable presence for her. In the early days of her therapy, Katie came to the sessions tentatively. It was as though she was poking her head round the corner first, to check that I was there. When I asked her about this, she said that she half expected me not to be there.

'Where would I be?'

'You might be ill.'

She worried about me and my ability to be there for her session after session.

After the first summer break, Katie did not turn up for her session, but I got a phone call to say that she was extremely ill in hospital. She had sustained a severe asthma attack. While she was in hospital and later at home, we kept in touch by telephone. It felt to me as though Katie was hanging on by a single thread and that I could very easily lose her. It was during this time that she said to me, 'I have a very strong pull towards *death*'. I also felt this pull in her. Later, I realised how the telephone had functioned as a symbolic umbilical cord between us, with Katie a tiny life fighting to stay alive and myself holding her and willing her to live. The sense that our connection was precarious and in some way also vital, was very strong. It subsequently became apparent that during that uncertain or vulnerable time, I was Katie's strong mother, willing and trusting this precariously attached tiny life to stay alive. Her acute illness at this time in her therapy had, I believe, thrown us back to her very early experience in the womb. As the therapy and our relationship evolved and deepened, I was to discover the truth of what I had sensed.

This brings me to what I want to say about prenatal and birth imprints in Katie which were brought to bear on our relationship. Katie's mother became pregnant with her a few months after losing a previous baby and her own mother. Even as I heard this, I felt it to be significant, but how it would affect Katie would not become clear until our work together was almost completed. Becoming pregnant so soon after a double loss meant that Katie's mother had been unable to truly mourn for her lost baby and her own mother. This was carried over into her new pregnancy, lacing it with fear and preventing a healthy attachment to her baby. When we are afraid of losing, we are afraid to love. She feared loving the new baby she had conceived in case it (he or she) would die, just as the other baby had done. This means that Katie was carried *in fear of death* and loss and that her mother was full of negative foreboding, harbouring such thoughts as *this one will die, too; they will all die; my mother is dead, there is no one there for me*. I have put these words in italics for a reason that will become clear later on in Katie's story.

When someone is unable, for whatever reason, to mourn a loss, then he or she cannot move on. The unresolved grief is carried in the heart as a wall of tears which makes it difficult if not impossible, to love again, until the pain has been released. Studies on the impact of previous perinatal loss on subsequent pregnancies highlight the susceptibility to complications in childbirth and successive attachment patterns. Losing a baby either before, during or after birth has been shown to affect a mother's bonding with a new baby, both before and after birth. This is not so difficult to understand, for it means that it is hard to let yourself fall in love again if you have sustained the loss of a loved one. In childbirth, it appears that such loss and unresolved grief may be inherited by women from their mothers and expressed as heightened anxiety during pregnancy.

Katie had inherited something of her mother's unresolved grief and fear of loss and death. Katie's mother was lonely, for her emotional relationship with her husband was at that time not satisfying. Whatever love she felt in her life, it was gone. This lonely woman conceived a new child, but it was hard for her to enjoy the new life growing inside her. It may be that at the time she was carrying Katie, part of her wanted to die too, to be with her own mother and baby. This was transmitted to Katie in the womb, so that today the grown up Katie says, '*All I ever had, everyone I love, is dead. I am left alone. I'm always being left.*' She is referring here to her brother and her father, but I believe that these are also her mother's words transmitted to her in the womb. The reader will remember the words I put in italics earlier. This means that death and abandonment had a particular emotional charge for Katie, as it may have for any of us wounded in that way.

Katie fears also that Rosie, her daughter, will die and then there will be no one left. Indeed, she fears that I will die. For some wounded part of Katie, death is a longed-for paradise state. It is oblivion, where all the loved ones await. Indeed death becomes preferable to life. I think that Katie's time in the womb instilled in her a particular fear of death, but also a very specific relationship to it and an ambivalent attitude to life. I think that she was undoubtedly influenced by her mother's thoughts and feelings in pregnancy and that this remained with her into post-womb life and beyond. If your mother who is carrying you and on whom you are totally dependent, thinks about death all the time and feels as if she wants to die, then what does this teach you when you are but a tiny life inside her?

Katie had, in her own words, a great pull towards death and this indeed was acted out after birth (when she almost died) and still is in Katie's life, since she has a number of times become seriously ill. The first major breakdown in her adult life (her lungs actually ceased to function and she was put on a ventilator) came after the birth of her daughter, which reactivated all her own prenatal and birth trauma. When things got too much for her, then she collapsed, or more specifically, her lungs appeared to collapse so that she was in threat of not being able to breathe.

Katie experienced Rose's birth as traumatic; it was long and arduous. She didn't know what was happening and she felt out of control and thought that she was dying. After the birth by forceps delivery, Katie could not cope with the baby and care for her in the normal way. She felt emotionally and physically drained and that the baby had sapped her strength. Eventually she was hospitalised for two or more months, hovering between life and death.

It is interesting to note that asthma and respiratory problems are symbolic of a fear or conflict about taking in life (breath). Katie was caught between living and dying. Dethlefsen's *The Healing Power of Illness,* which examines the psychological and symbolic meaning of illness in the individual, explains the psychological component of asthma. He suggests that because breathing is a rhythmic activity, it is a good example of the law of polarity, breathing in/breathing out. The constantly alternating poles of inspiration and expiration go to make up a rhythm. Each pole owes its life to the existence of the other, its opposite; doing away with the one you do away with the other. Life/Death, living/dying and so on.

Explaining that asthma more specifically is to do with the constriction of the small bronchi and bronchioles during expiration, Dethlefsen suggests that asthmatics are so frightened of not getting enough that they are trying to take too much in.

They breathe so deeply that they over-inflate the lungs, so producing a cramp when they breathe out. This means that they cannot let go of what they have used.[1]

Katie always complains about her chest being tight and Dethlefsen notes that, in Greek, asthma is referred to as 'tight chestedness'. 'In Latin the word for 'tight' is *angustus*, to which the word "anxiety" is closely related. In German, meanwhile, the words *angst* (fear, anxiety) and *eng* (tight, narrow) are inseparably linked.'[2] Thus the tightness that is characteristic of asthma has a great deal to do with fear: the fear of taking in life. It could be said that death represents in asthmatics the ultimate opportunity to shut themselves off from the world of the living – perhaps a world that has become unbearable because it is fraught with pain, difficulties and choices that appear insurmountable. Katie told me that when her elderly mother was ill and upset, she would say to Katie that she was only living for her, but that she wanted to die. In therapy, Katie cried as she tells me she is not worth living for.

When we do not have a secure sense of self, we often project aspects of ourselves of which we are unaware onto other people in our lives. These people, often partners or close friends, then embody those parts for us. We feel that we cannot do without them and so if the relationship breaks down, then we are desolate. Jung discovered that there exists in the psyche of every man an inner woman, called the anima and in every woman an inner man, the animus. As the fundamental forms which underlie the 'feminine' aspects of man and the 'masculine' aspects of woman, they are seen as opposites. Jung described them as soul images. These images are not gender related, rather they are universal forces in every man and every woman. The anima and animus, as inner soul images, guide our creative spirit and are responsible for how we relate to the opposite sex.

Since Katie had a very frail sense of self, she tended to project her creative energy into male partners like John who have money and power. These animus figures either died like her brother, or were emotionally unavailable and addictive per-

157

sonalities like John. Katie's brother was strong and had nurtured and protected her. He was a positive masculine figure for her and his death left her bereft and lonely. Whilst he was alive, Katie could feel nurtured and cared for when she was with him, but once he left her, she felt alone. She was not only without an outer man, she was without an inner man. So that if her love relationship broke down, she had no inner man to fall back on and so was bereft. Though to an extent she had projected animus onto John, when they split up, she was alone again. When Katie came to therapy first, she used to have a recurring dream:

I go to a little house, a cottage. It is very pretty with flowers around it. I am going to visit my brother who has been there for five years. An elderly woman is there and she says that he has gone away – something about the war. I enter the house and spend ages looking in all the rooms, opening the doors and calling his name. But they are empty and there is no one there.

I felt that the dream was showing me how Katie's 'house' (the psyche, symbolic of Katie herself) was empty. No sense of self dwelt there (although it was pretty on the outside). In the dream Katie is looking everywhere for her brother but he is gone. He represented her inner man; he had died and she was now empty.

I think the five years to be significant. This is how old Katie was when her brother was born. Perhaps the dream image of the empty cottage represented at another level her mother, empty and barren before the birth of her son. A house can also represent the body and dreams of an empty house can not only represent loneliness and loss at a psychic level but also a physical sense of being infertile or 'empty', without the creative spirit. Katie says that her brother was her strength. He was the wind beneath her wings. She loved him and without him she had nothing. Her mother felt so too, constantly reminding her daughter of how delicate and small she was and how strong her brother was. He was encouraged to be creative and an achiever. Katie, by contrast, was told that she was too delicate to be able to achieve much in life and was taught to be dependent. She grew up feeling that she had nothing. The men had it, though; it was in money and power and social position.

Katie's earliest experiences and her internalisation of her mother's own mental representations of what it is to be a woman and a mother, meant that the feminine was entirely devalued in the family. Everything good, strong and creative was projected into the masculine. Today, the adult Katie feels herself to be incapable of creative action and her dream images and the stories they tell reflect her propensity to project all her creativity into men who do not then care for her, or who leave her. She is always left empty.

I believe that Katie suffered considerable maternal deprivation in the womb. Her mother was in a way emotionally unavailable to her. Impingement is a term used by Winnicott to describe a situation where the infant's development is hampered by the mother's own preoccupations which renders her unavailable to the child. I do not know what Katie's mother was feeling when she discovered that she was pregnant with her, but it seems likely that she was still in grief and preoccupied with the death and loss of her own mother and first baby. These preoccupations left her unable to enter into and share her baby's experience, beyond hoping and wishing the new baby to live.

Katie's prenatal experience left her no space to develop a sense of herself. She felt that she had nothing and was nothing except what her mother wished her to be. It felt to me at that time, that at the deepest level, Katie's mother did not really emotionally *expect* her new baby during her pregnancy, being too preoccupied with her recent losses. This, I believe, accounts for Katie's sense of no self and for my sense in her of an emptiness. It also accounts for her compliant self and for the part of her that is totally identified with her mother and with me in her therapy. Lack of mourning means the inability to acknowledge separation in a relationship since this involves having to bear the pain of the potential loss of the loved one. If one is identified with the loved one, however, then the pain of separation and potential loss is avoided. I found that Katie expressed this in her need to cut off from anything she felt was too painful to be suffered emotionally, so that when things became difficult for her in her life outside therapy or in her relationship with me, she was compelled to take breaks by going away on holidays. This was her way of looking after herself and treating her chesty condition by resting and breathing better air.

Mourning is necessary for creativity and growth and denial of the pain of loss leads to insecure attachment patterns and dependence. Katie's mother's inability to properly mourn the death of her baby and her own mother all those years before left her helpless and dependent and unable to enter joyously into her new pregnancy with Katie. In therapy and in her life, it was possible to see in Katie the legacy of her mother and the chains of unresolved grief carried perhaps from many generations.

After birth, Katie was delicate and her mother was unable to care for her because she herself was sick. Katie told me that her mother could not handle it when she was ill; it was her father who used to care for her and visit her in hospital. Terrified of losing her second baby, Katie's mother overprotected her child. Katie told me that she was mollycoddled and breast fed up until she was five years old and her brother was born. Her mother kept her very close, being afraid lest anything should happen to her. Mother and baby were one. Katie's mother saw her baby daughter as an extension of herself, which meant that it was difficult for Katie to develop her own sense of self.

Emotionally unavailable mothers tend to produce in their children difficulties in relationships, particularly at an intimate level. When such children become adults, they are prone to perpetuate similar attachment patterns with others. When Katie did become ill, her mother simply appeared to detach herself, unable to contain her own pain and anxiety. She distanced herself from her child, so that Katie experienced this as her mother never being reliably available for her. When there is fear of loss, there is difficulty in loving. Fear of suffering also hardens the heart and it is so hard to open to love when we are frightened. This pattern was being repeated by Katie with her own daughter; she was over-identified with her as a defence against separation and loss, but she also detached from Rosie, finding it difficult to handle difficult emotional situations. If Rosie was upset or ill, Katie found it very hard to stay with her daughter.

A similar situation would happen in therapy, in that when things would get difficult emotionally, Katie often felt compelled to go away. This was her way of proving to herself that she did not really need me, or at any rate she was not dependent on me. The fear of and defence against getting too close emotionally, must have been exactly what Katie's mother did when she discovered she was pregnant with her.

It is almost inevitable that women who have lost a baby will feel like this, since they will unconsciously protect themselves from loss. Katie's mother, too, was protecting herself from loving her baby in case she would lose her. The loss would be too great to be borne. Katie's brother was strong and healthy and Harriet felt her mother favoured him over her. He was her strong son, never ill, not like delicate little Katie. Yet he too was to die. When Katie came to me first, she would say that she felt her mother really thought or wished that she (Katie) should have been the one to have died. I think that a part of Katie felt the same. They were very close, she said; he was almost a part of her and when he died she felt that a part of her had gone. Without him she was nothing.

Katie had great anxiety about separation, which I feel has much to do with the aloneness of the baby in the womb who is unsure if it is wanted. I think that the combination of her mother's fear of becoming attached to her unborn baby for fear of losing her and also paradoxically her wish that she live, produced in Harriet this ambivalence towards life. Part of her wanted to live and part of her wanted to die. To me, it almost feels as though this little baby had no one to bond with, either before or after birth. Janov tells us that patients report this birth feeling in adult life as an overwhelming emptiness, coupled with a chronic anxiety.[3]

161

Separation anxiety is frequently at the bottom of compulsive behaviour. People who feel that inner emptiness often become compulsive in an effort to rid themselves of the feeling. Many women are aware, for example, of over eating when they feel depressed or stressed. Others, often men, will bury themselves in their work, still others will exercise compulsively. Katie needed to constantly fill herself up with parties, expensive dinners, champagne and anything that money could buy as a means of filling or hiding that emptiness. But she also knew that this did not really fulfil her. In therapy, Katie often needed to phone or write to me, as well as coming to her sessions. It was as though in order to feel 'connected' to me she had to maintain a concrete link. After a break of therapy, no matter how short, Katie would invariably appear distant from me, her voice barely audible and it would take time before I felt a connection between us. She would appear particularly childlike after these breaks and not emotionally available. As a young child Katie was often left alone and separated from her mother to go into hospital. As an adult she had a fear of abandonment, a stark terror even of being left alone. I think this was the raw terror of the baby separated from her mother. But I would go further and say that it was also an expression of fear of the unknown, of insecurity in the face of abandonment.

Katie also had a fear of the dark and more specifically of falling asleep, which is most certainly connected with an acute fear of death in all its forms. At one level, I feel that she was suffering gravely from that dark period just before she saw the light of day. It seems that dark represents agony and light represents respite—for it was in the light that the agony (of birth) stopped. It was in the light that breathing began. It was in the light that life (after birth) began. Indeed it was in the light that it became apparent that the struggle (to come into the world) had been successful. At another level, Katie's fear of the dark was her fear of the unknown, of the black night of the soul, of helplessness in the midst of chaos, of the pain of abandonment.

We worked together for a long time and things slowly began to change. I felt that in time, Katie was much more able to be with herself, which is the result of finally being able to internalise a good mother. She was able, by the end of therapy, to have and to hold a positive inner mother, which means that she is not now alone. And *there is someone there for her.* This happened because our relationship was strong enough for Katie to begin to have and to hold a sense of her own worth. She gradually became less compelled to phone or check that I was there, trusting more that I *was there.* For Katie, the important thing was our emotional bond and the feeling that I cared for her and she me. Indeed it took a very long time for this to happen and be acknowledged by her.

Where originally the therapy and her commitment to it had been experienced by Katie as confining and demanding of her time, it became something which she felt was truly there for her in whatever way she needed. I became less the impinging mother making demands on her and more the mother who was there for her. My part had been simply to *be there* consistently and doggedly, trusting that both she and I would survive. Part of this meant that I had to allow her to do what she had needed to do, in order to test me to see if I would go, or leave her, or die. It meant that I had to be there, no matter what. Sensing and being able to accept that I cared for her, enabled her to value herself enough to distinguish love from money and to desire the former. Perhaps the experience of unconditional love was not something which she had encountered and this made it difficult for her to have a sense of her own worth.

Notes

1.   T. Dethlefsen *The Healing Power of Illness.* (Element Books, 1990), p. 114.
2.   ibid., p. 119.

Chapter Ten

Birth Revisited

'Our birth is but a sleep and a forgetting:
the soul that rises with us, our life's star,
hath had elsewhere its setting
and cometh from afar.'
(Wordsworth Ode, *Intimations of Immortality*
from Recollections of Early Childhood)

'I'm afraid I might die,' the woman said as she clutched in terror at the therapist's hands.

'You won't let me die will you?' she beseeched.

The therapist, experienced with this sort of reaction, gently reassured her and settled her down on the mat. She felt cold, she said, so he covered her with a blanket. Holding her hand, he urged her to breathe deeply and to focus on what was happening inside her. It wasn't long before the young woman, dizzy and nauseated, began her journey into a place she'd never imagined existed. At once she found herself in a long, black corridor. It was suffocating. It was hot and stuffy. Throwing off the blanket, she thrashed about, her body twisting this way and that, panic beginning to rise.

'I need to get out, I need to get out,' she screamed and found herself then underground it seemed and flying down a chute of water. Suddenly there were lots and lots of colours rainbow like and the sounds of music. She would have liked to stay but it was all hurrying by so fast. Wait, wait she thought. Then the cave became dark and gloomy with something in the corner; it was not good. It felt bad and evil there. Then the bats appeared overhead and she felt trapped again. She screamed, 'let me out, I've got to get out.'

She ran along faster and faster but she was getting nowhere. She couldn't get out, it was too far – too far. She reached out at a hanging root that seemed to be against the wall, now wet and slimy. It became the umbilical cord. She tugged and tugged, but it was no good

'I'm going to die in here, no-one knows I'm here. Don't forget I'm in here.'

Suddenly she went quiet, her body limp and damp, perspiration on her neck and chest.

'What's happening now?' the therapist asks after a long pause.

No answer.

'Where are you?

'I feel tired now, I feel sleepy. I don't want to do this anymore.'

'Who's saying this?'

'My mother. My mother is saying this. She's tired. She feels she can't go on. It's taking so long, I'm so tired. I don't care any more, I'm going to die. I'm going to die I have no energy left. It's going to be too late. The baby will be dead.'

These are her mother's words transmitted to her in the womb. Her mother was in labour, but haemorrhaging badly. It was an emergency and the baby had no chance of life unless an immediate caesarean took place. Weak from shock and loss of blood, her mother lapsed into a desperate lethargy. After a long ride to the hospital, sedation and a general anaesthetic, the baby was delivered. She was very small, suffering from oxygen deprivation and had difficulty breathing.

Suddenly the woman screamed again and pulled away from the therapist, her body assuming a curled up fetal position. She seemed to be crouching away from something.

'What's happening?'

'No- no- no.' She began to cry.

'What is it?'

'They are cutting the box. They don't know I'm in there. They will cut me too. Don't cut me. My mother is gone, she's dead, but I'm not dead, I'm still alive I'm alone in here. There is no one there.'

She found herself huddled in a tiny space and could hear voices. There were people approaching. There was a sense of panic again and great fear. She crouched away from them and making herself as small as possible, pulled her legs up underneath her.

'I don't want to come out, but I have to, otherwise I will die.'

She experienced the crushing conflict between life and death impulses and overwhelmingly, the powerlessness of her position. There was no escape and nowhere to go.

She relived the first few moments after birth as intensely charged. Her body felt like a bundle of raw nerves. Electric shocks ran through her. She cried out but caught her breath. There wasn't much time and she hadn't much energy. She couldn't move much and when she did, it hurt. The thing they stuck in her throat hurt. She gagged and gagged. The pain in her throat grew worse.

'Leave me alone, leave me alone.'

She lay there, she wanted to sleep.

It grew quiet in the room – only the sound of her breathing and the scratching of the therapist's pen could be heard. It reassured her. It was safe.

Starting up again, she began to cough and then choke and clutching her throat she spluttered, trying to speak. He bent to hear the words.

'I can't breathe,' she gasped.

'What's happening?' asks the therapist.

'They're here'

'Who's here? What are they doing to you?'

'They are trying to feed me, but I can't, I can't, it hurts.' She rasped, clutching at her throat again.

She was in the incubator, re-experiencing the nasal-gastric tube feeding. Her system, too immature to cope with feeding and breathing at the same time, was in total revolt. This merged with later memories of choking and meant that for a timeless moment she experienced the conflict between feeding and breathing. Taking in nourishment meant not being able to breathe. She could not do both. Each feed left her gasping and choking for air. She just wanted them to leave her alone.

Later, much later it seemed, a woman appeared, surrounded by white light. She had a beautiful wise face and she wore a cloak. An aura of peace and serenity filled the room. She touched the baby gently and instantly the child felt warm and safe. A soft glow seemed to be all around her and the woman told her not to be afraid.

'Have courage. You have a lot to do here. You are needed to work with the women in the family.'

'You are helping ·heal the wounds of aeons of women, wounds to the heart, wounds of love.'

From inside her cloak the wise woman produced a gift; it was a stone in the shape of a heart. It shone and reflected many colours. It was to be kept with her at all times. Behind the wise woman there appeared a black wolf. His eyes were kind and he came and sat protectively beside her. She was a woman herself now, feeling strong and full of light. The pain in her body was gone and she felt peaceful.

The therapist rustled his papers and as the woman felt herself return to the therapy room, she was filled with a sense of awe and purpose. She was no longer afraid. She was calm and serene. She lay there for some time.

The above represents fragments of a personal account of a birth regression session. Though unique to the person who experienced it, it contains many elements which are common to those who relive their prenatal and birth experience. Common to most is a sense of fear and panic and increasingly reported, is the feeling of alienation and aloneness the baby encounters as a response to the mother's anaesthesia during labour and birth. An anaesthetised mother cannot help her baby into life and if she is distressed herself, she cannot reassure her child. Some babies experience this as though their mother were dead and a baby, unlike its mother, will not know that there is an end to the struggle. Reassurance during any major life event which is experienced as stressful or traumatic is something everyone will seek. A baby, however, lacking as yet the cognitive capacity to understand that his or her ordeal will eventually be over, is even more vulnerable and completely helpless.

This experience will influence the baby's later psychological development. It may produce reactive behaviour such as becoming caretaker to the mother, or compensatory behaviour, such as becoming powerful and controlling in an attempt to overcome a sense of helplessness. The fear and a pervading sense of being alone or abandoned may lace that child's relationships in later life. The emotional imprints of the birth trauma are generally reactivated and reinforced by later life experiences. Most of us will form defences against a sense of helplessness and abandonment and so we will try very hard to avoid having to experience this again. But since life is a teacher, it is in the nature of things, that unwittingly, we will create situations in our lives where we have to face the very thing we are avoiding.

Pre and perinatal psychotherapy often involves working more experientially than the purely cognitive approach of analytical psychotherapy. This may involve breathing techniques, or the use of music and visualisation to induce a deeply relaxed state, which will enable the emergence of images and memories from the depths of the psyche. Prenatal and birth experiences represent a deep layer of the unconscious which is largely inaccessible to more verbal approaches. Birth wounds are generally hidden in the more primitive, feeling layers of the psyche. At the deepest level, it is the body which carries these memories and so it is through feeling states that the pain is released. This means that some form of bodywork, massage or movement for example, will be a necessary part of healing. The body, which has been the register of what the mind has not been capable of handling, will need gentle urging in order to release its hidden secrets. Often, other physical experiences such as illness or childbirth for example, will release memories of past trauma.

Although there has been a strong interest in the relation of psyche to soma (mind/body) throughout the development of psychological understanding in the past century, little of this has permeated conventional psychoanalytic psychotherapy. This has led to a regrettable division between humanistic therapies (which involve the body) and psychoanalytic psychotherapy (the mind). An integration of methods has become necessary particularly within the area of prenatal and birth experiences. True healing at a somatic as well as a psychic level, can only take place if such an integration happens in the wounded individual. Often physical sensations may emerge during a regression which indicate a energetic or body release and this forms part of the healing process. Alexander Lowen knew this well when he said, 'Knowledge becomes understanding when it is coupled with feeling.'

In this chapter we will be looking at regression therapy as a method of working with prenatal and birth material. The wounds of birth are deep wounds, wounds buried in a most primitive layer of the psyche and healing these wounds often involves work at a pre-verbal or body level, beyond the reach of classical psychoanalytical methods. In a model of expanded human consciousness, which includes altered or non-ordinary states, it is possible to relive biological birth and the prenatal state. This reactivation to a reliving of biological birth is the basis of birth regression therapy. It allows individuals to not only access suppressed memories, but also to experience their emotional responses to specific traumas which then become blueprints for behavioural patterns in their adult lives.

Birth as Soul Experience

Seeing birth as a soul experience means accepting the transpersonal dimension of life. It means acknowledging and embracing a necessarily spiritual perspective to human experiences such as birth. Much of birth regression work is consequently conducted against a background of expanded human consciousness. It is worth looking at the history and background against which birth can be seen as a soul experience.

Expanded Human Consciousness

Modern research in the area of human consciousness has necessitated a shift in belief structures. Whereas formerly, it was generally thought that consciousness was created by and limited to the human brain, now it is seen as something that exists outside and independent of us, although we form part of it. Consciousness in its essence is not bound to matter and the human psyche has no boundaries or limits. Stanislav Grof, pioneer in transpersonal psychology and the author of many books on the subject suggests that, 'If we accept this new view of consciousness, it means accepting also that our lives are not shaped only by the immediate environmental influences since the day of our birth but, of at least equal importance, they are shaped by ancestral, cultural, spiritual and cosmic influences beyond the scope of what we can perceive with our physical senses'.[1] New scientific discoveries mean that we are seeing the emergence of a new, much broader image of the psyche.

Jung, in his acceptance of the objectivity of the psyche, had set a precedent. In *Seven Sermons of the Dead*, first published in 1916, Jung describes transpersonal experiences which were to deeply influence his work. There, he began communicating with a spirit being who called himself 'Philemon.' In his observations about the workings and scope of the human psyche, Jung concluded that Philemon had taught him 'psychic objectivity, the reality of the psyche.' He explained the ability of the psyche to record and remember experiences which went far beyond the confines of biography, through his concepts of the collective unconscious and the existence of archetypes which informed our minds and governed our behaviour. These are universal forces, or sources of energy that exist in their own right and that influence mankind.

Birth Revisited

Psychological Death and Rebirth

An example is the birth archetype. Death and rebirth are fundamental principles that affect us all. Jung saw how psychologically, rebirth became possible through an encounter with the archetype of transformation, a process which happened naturally in the psyche through individuation. The concepts of death and rebirth have always been with us and in many ancient and advanced cultures, people were able to experience the sacred mysteries through transformation rites based on specific mythologies and representing important elements of life in ancient civilisations. In Babylonia, for example, death and rebirth rites were held in the name of Ishtar and Tammuz; in Egypt it was Isis and Osiris. We have, as examples too, the Elusinian mysteries of ancient Greece (Demeter and Persephone), and the Dionysian rites. In antiquity, many important cultural and political figures such as Plato and Aristotle were initiates of these mysteries.

In Jungian psychology, the symbolic death and surrender of the ego, such as in a mental breakdown, leads to a rebirth of personality, to a whole more integrated sense of oneself. This new personality is called the Self. But death of the ego alarms many of us, for it brings with it the fear of isolation from others, alienation from oneself and ultimately, madness. On the other hand, death is implicit to the concept of transformation. We can observe this in nature and all natural processes, where regeneration involves a process of death and rebirth, the old giving birth to the new and so on. On a personal level, depressions and mental breakdowns represent the possibility of psychological death and rebirth. This means that for a time, part of us must break down or die, for it is only in the death that a rebirth becomes possible. We can recognise this at those times when we have to make a difficult choice or decision, which usually means having to let go of something. We know at some level that until we do that, the new cannot be born, whether it be a choice of career, partner, or other important part of our lives. Surrender involves a sacrifice and it is this that makes the transformation possible. D.H. Lawrence wrote of the death-rebirth struggle:

Are you willing to be sponged out, erased, cancelled,
made nothing?
Are you willing to be made nothing?
dipped into oblivion?

If not, you will never really change.

(D.H. Lawrence, Phoenix)

On a spiritual level, the symbolism of rebirth is often used
as a metaphor for initiation into higher conscious awareness or
spirituality. In order to achieve wholeness, an old way of being
has to die. This is not always an easy task, since it means letting
go of what we have previously known. Unsure, part of us will
hold back when offered the opportunity to change our lives.
Fearing the step into the unknown, we want reassurances that
where we are going is right for us. But there are no reassurances
in death, which involves a process of surrender to forces greater
than ourselves. The idea that one must die in order to be reborn
is found also in the writings and teachings of the mystics, which
takes the form of letting go of ego attachments or desire, in
order to reach wisdom and enlightenment. The mystics speak
of the daily dying to the self.

Birth Memories

Since transpersonal psychology presupposes different psychic
realities, the idea that one can relive or re-experience one's prenatal and birth experience in the context of regression therapy
is not difficult to accept. It is now possible to access human
experiences or memories which formerly lay firmly hidden, it
was believed, beneath the layers of the primitive unconscious.
Explorations with non-ordinary states of consciousness has provided convincing evidence that we do store memories of birth,
prenatal and even earlier experiences in our psyches, at a deep
cellular level. People with no conscious knowledge of the particular circumstances surrounding their births have been able to
remember and relive, with astounding detail, facts concerning
their births, such as type of delivery and also their mothers'

thoughts and feeling responses during her pregnancy. These details have been checked and objectively confirmed in the vast majority of cases.

Grof, psychiatrist as well as author, contends that most of the fundamental symptoms of mental illness can be explained by making specific reference to the birth process. Describing his work, he reported that all his patients experienced psychological death and rebirth during LSD induced regressions. With time and as the experiences became more familiar to him, he concluded that what he was witnessing were normal and natural manifestations of the deepest domains of the human psyche. Furthermore, when the process moved beyond the biographical material from infancy and childhood and the experiences began to reveal the greater depths of the human psyche, the therapeutic results improved. Symptoms that had resisted months or even years of treatment often vanished after patients had experiences such as psychological death and rebirth.[2]

Grof focused on the reliving of the prenatal and birth experience. These experiences were formative in that they created imprints which influenced future behaviour. What is important is that Grof found that entering and experiencing the trauma of birth, we encounter a strange intertwining of birth and death, as if these two aspects of the human experience were somehow one. Along with a sense of life-threatening confinement comes a determined struggle to free oneself and survive. In reliving our biological births, we have experiences of an archetypal nature and we confront the death/rebirth archetype. We tap into deeper sources in our psyche. We tap into the collective unconscious at a very direct level. Grof found that perinatal memories provide us with a doorway into the collective unconscious.

My own experiences and observations in the field of birth regression have led me to the conclusion that birth and the prenatal experience is seminal to the future development of human life and further that memories of these experiences remain with us as inner images which form part of the way we live our lives. Archetypal experiences convinced me not only of the existence of the collective unconscious, a vast pool of primordial experience which was recorded somewhere in the darkest recess of our psyches and which informed our lives, but also of the possibility of having experienced past lives. These experiences taught me much of the power and depth of the human psyche and its abilities to lift us far beyond the confines of our mortality.

The Soul's Journey: Reincarnation

Many of those working with birth regression do so against a background of Eastern religious thought, karmic philosophy and reincarnation, in which birth is a biological rebirth into one life amongst many. In this way, life is a continuum which transgresses the boundaries of our biological existence. Sogyal Rinpoche, Tibetan spiritual leader, who authored *The Tibetan Book of Living and Dying* confirms that, 'since the dawn of history, reincarnation and a firm faith in life after death have occupied an essential place in nearly all the world's religions'.[3] Belief in rebirth existed among Christians in the early history of Christianity and persisted in various forms well into the Middle Ages. Origen, one of the most influential of the church fathers, believed in the pre-existence of souls. And although Christianity eventually rejected the belief in reincarnation, traces of it can be found throughout Renaissance thought and in the writings of major romantic poets like Wordsworth, as quoted at the beginning of the chapter. Many westerners have now come to believe in the Buddhist doctrine of reincarnation. Within this belief, biological birth is merely a transitional state, that is a BAR-DO state, which means a state between lifetimes. In order to fully understand this, let us look briefly at the concepts of karma and reincarnation.

Both these concepts are fundamental to all eastern religions. They are inextricably linked and one without the other renders them meaningless. Karma refers to the universal law of cause and effect. It is identical with the biblical idea that, 'Whatsoever a man soweth, that shall he also reap' or 'An eye for an eye and a tooth for a tooth.' It is ultimately infinite in scope since it embraces a time span which is continuous over many lifetimes but at the same time maintains an equanimity of universal justice and equilibrium. In other words, the most important aspect of this law is the law of adjustment. The actual root meaning of *karma* in sanskrit means action and refers to the continuous self adjusting dynamic that pervades all existence. It ultimately forces us to take responsibility for our own actions. Karma is the actual fuel that feeds the fire of rebirth and all Eastern religions have developed a technology whose prime aim is to reduce and dissolve the effects of this fuel which impels us ever headlong into the cycle of rebirth. In the Buddhist tradition the goal of liberation techniques and spiritual practices is called 'Nirvana' which has been interpreted in numerous ways but whose literal meaning is 'where the wind of Karma does not blow'.

Bardo is a word much popularised by the translation of the *Tibetan Book of the Dead,* first translated by Evan-Wentz in imitation of the *Egyptian Book of the Dead.* In a modern commentary, basically addressed to the Western World, Chogyam Trungpa Rinpoche calls it 'The Tibetan Book of Birth', thereby making the point that birth and death are fundamental principles that recur constantly in this life. Birth is always an initiation into another state and from the Eastern point of view indicates only a transition into another life amongst many.

In the idea of the Bardo, we can recognise the notion of the intermediary twilight level of consciousness, or the twilight period at sunset or dawn, when day turns into night and vice versa. These are borderline states. They are times of being neither in one thing or another, when change can most readily occur. Inherent to such states is the opportunity for transformation. So it is with the birth experience. In the crack between the two worlds of the living and the dead, or death and rebirth, lies the supreme opportunity for liberation.

Some pre and perinatal psychologists believe that the prenatal period, or the time in the womb, is an intermediary state between lives. Many believe in the existence of past lives and the principle of karma and that the unborn child chooses its parents for its own karmic reasons. Many souls come in to complete karmic business and therefore choose a particular mother and particular parents who will help them do this. Some therapists, like Roger Woolger, author of *Other Lives, Other Selves* have found that the perinatal experience interfaces with that of past life and that what happens in the womb is already scripted by past life experiences of life and death. Morris Netherton, in *Past Life Therapy*, proposed that the prenatal experience is of supreme importance in that, 'It is the only prolonged time when the unconscious mind functions alone, unaided by consciousness.' and that:

'The unborn child, awaiting the beginning of conscious life, is profoundly affected by his prenatal awareness. With no conscious to discern or interpret, the unconscious plays back any past-life incidences triggered by events in the mother's life. These incidences shape the behaviour patterns of the child. At birth the infant will begin a life of trying to resolve those past-life events without ever knowing what they are.'

As a result of this, Netherton contends that it is essential for a patient to work through his prenatal experience in order to deal with what past-life events may be influencing his current life. Netherton's contentions suggest that the prenatal period in every case contains the central core of the psychological complex at work in the life of the patient. He writes:

'In this embryonic space the rules of the game, so to speak, are set up for us. The issues that will confront us throughout conscious life are introduced and the 'memory' of certain past life traumas is locked into position. Then, just as this preamble is fully assembled, it is made inaccessible by the entrance of the conscious mind, at birth'.[4]

Regression Therapy

Whatever the particular belief, the prenatal and birth experience is considered of supreme importance, for it is here that many patterns are laid down which will have a bearing on later behaviour and life experience. Pre and perinatal psychologists believe that by accessing and reliving memories and emotional thought patterns of that time, one can become free of them. It is on this basis that most advocate a reliving or a reactivation of suppressed memories and emotional responses during the pre-natal and birth period, in order to fully achieve psychological health and integration of personality.

Freud suggested that the prenatal state was characterised by an 'oceanic feeling of bliss' that invoked a wish to return to the womb. Otto Rank also held this view. But the more recent findings of many therapists suggest that on the contrary, the womb is a place where patterns of distress that were later to emerge in childhood, are formed. Furthermore, it appears that for some, the prenatal state simply reflects traumatic incidents that have been initiated in former lifetimes. In a book entitled *Regression Therapy: A Handbook for Professionals*, W.B. Lucas draws together leading therapists in the field of regression therapy. The book contains essays in extended areas of altered state work, including prenatal and birth regression. Irene Hickman, physician and hypnotherapist, writes of the birth experience:

'Few patients find birth something they look forward to eagerly. The more common reaction is regret, reluctance and even refusal. Birth in a sense promises blood, sweat, tears and an endless chain of choices.'[5]

An important discovery, is that the fetus in the womb is like a tape recorder, recording all the mother's thoughts and feelings. And furthermore, that as there is no discerning ego to filter this, it takes all these as its own. The fetus is unable to distinguish between what belongs to it and what belongs to its mother. This means that in the womb we take on as it were, the dramas of our parents. It has been found that the fetus also records words and that these may be its mother's words transmitted to it in the womb.

Another finding of regression therapy is that fear is an emotion which, especially if it is persistent in the mother prenatally, but also if it is present at and during the birth, will pervade the unborn baby, who again experiences it as his or her own. When intense fear is chronic in a person it can very often be traced back to the prenatal period and may originate as the mother's fear. This fear can become amplified during the delivery and can sometimes be found to originate in the medical team attending the birth.[6] Alice Givens makes the point that the strongest imprints in the form of messages from the mother occur during the prenatal and birth experiences because there is no escape from them.

Releasing The Feelings

Therapists differ in their method of contacting prenatal and birth experiences. Most therapists will use feeling states to expand and deepen such memories rather than depend on a cognitive approach. Many will use images that arise spontaneously from the client and amplify these in order to facilitate the emergence of unconscious memories. The therapist will usually work with the client's right brain in order to bypass the controlling, rational left brained ego. The right brain is more primitive and the seat of feeling, intuition and psychic awareness. Generally, we use the right brain when we are being spontaneous, loving and creative and we use the left brain to rationalise and give order to our lives. If we are working well with both sides of us, then we will use the left brain to harness the creativity emanating from our intuitive, feeling side. Often though, we will suppress our feelings and intuition in favour of our rational minds, because we have been taught, by and large, to be suspicious of anything which we cannot control.

The person who has regressed to a true prenatal or birth state will be so totally involved in the feeling or memory of that time that he or she will not be rationalising. Often the scene will have to be replayed again and again, until the pent up energy has been fully released and the client can then begin the work of healing the experience. Some therapists, including myself, believe that traumatic experiences must be fully lived through on a somatic and emotional level in order for healing to take place. It will not be enough to merely recover prenatal and birth memories; knowing about it doesn't change the feelings. The aim of regression therapy is to enable clients to gain access to unconscious memories and trauma which are affecting their lives and behaviour and which are located way back in the person's life, sometimes prenatal, birth and as we have seen, even further back, to past life experiences. Releasing the trauma, by reliving it within the safe containment of the therapeutic situation, leads to being able to let it go. Trauma that is stored in the unconscious mind contains energy and as it is relived and expressed, that energy is released, whether it relates to childhood, infancy, or prenatal and birth memories.

The brain creates its own anaesthesia, so that when suffering becomes unbearable, there is a blanking, a cutting off mechanism which comes into play as a protection. In psychological language this is called splitting off. In the practice of regression therapy, this means that when the trauma becomes too great to be borne, the client will go out of his or her body. People often experience this as being outside and above their bodies, observing and looking down on it, as it were. In this way, the person can observe what is going on from a safe distance but cannot feel the feelings. This psychic state is very similar to what people describe when they are recounting traumatic out of body experiences, such as consciousness during major surgery, or accidents, or near-death experiences.

During deep regression work, if it feels appropriate to aid the release of a hidden trauma and enable a client to feel, techniques such as deep breathing and body work and the presence and skill of the therapist will be necessary. Ever mindful of protecting the integrity of a wounded person, the unconscious mind will allow the original experience to come into awareness only under conditions that it perceives as safe. It has always been my practice to trust the inherent wisdom of the unconscious, so that, if the resistances are too great in the client at a particular time, then they must be respected. It often needs time for deeply buried wounds to be made conscious and for a healing to take place. Paying particular attention to dreams and spontaneous images will often indicate what needs to happen and will be a guideline as to how to proceed when a person appears to be blocked.

I have found that the psyche will often spontaneously produce in image form, guide figures and similar helpers who will, by virtue of being connected to the person's Higher Self, act as protection. The simplest way of explaining this is that it appears that when a trauma, or the potential suffering involved in the uncovering of it, is very great, there will be at play in the psyche an inner guide or helper. In regression work, as in any other therapy, the therapist may sometimes hold or contain this for the client, or the therapeutic encounter itself will activate within the client the archetype of wisdom and healing. This is activated through what Jung termed the transcendent function. I believe that a conviction on the part of the therapist, of the existence in the human psyche, as in the body, of an innate healer that is always ready to be put into motion and to respond to the right conditions, is necessary in order to activate healing.

Telling the Story

I think it is unwise to assume that the remembering and the reliving alone, within the context of regression therapy, is enough to enable a person to be able to gain freedom from crippling emotional patterns. We may remember terrible incidents in our past which have caused us tremendous pain and which have been the cause of certain behavioural patterns in our lives. We may face our fear and relive these terrifying moments; we may release the pent up energy stored by these memories in our bodies, but at some profound level we must also understand them. And we can understand them only if we can give them meaning in our lives. This means that the wounded soul must be allowed to tell its story. Every soul wound has a story. A soul's story may be told in dreams, fantasies or other psychic activity, or it may be told in the body through physical symptoms. Once the story has begun, it should be allowed to flow and if possible, to be given form. This may take the form of writing, painting, sculpting or other creative activity.

Those that express concern that a technique which involves the reliving of distressing incidents may cause a psychotic breakdown, have a point. Though I do not necessarily agree with the cognitive approach which shies away from cathartic release during regression, I nonetheless feel strongly that unless such experiences can be fully integrated, usually through further cognitive, creative, non verbal or verbal techniques, such deep work can be not only distressing but in the long run, unproductive. Without the help and containment of a therapist, the client may not know what to do with what he or she has exposed.

It usually happens that once the work of uncovering the deepest layers of the psyche has begun, it will continue and may be given expression in nightmares, dreams and distressing physical symptoms. A strong and stable ego is necessary in order to be able to withstand the storm stirred up by unearthing the unconscious. Those with a stronger sense of self may cope well with what emerges from the dark side of the soul and indeed the work of healing may continue naturally within them. Some may have already developed techniques which they may use to help the inner healing process. For others, one or two sessions may be enough to release and transform previous destructive patterns.

In my experience though, this is not generally the case, for we are always learning and once we have begun to uncover the layers of experience formerly dormant in the psyche, the process continues, as one layer exposes another and so on. Moreover, the work of releasing and transforming do not necessarily happen together. For many, birth regression may be the beginning of a journey, for others it may be the catalyst to the end; the energy drive of each person is different, just as each individual's process is unique.

The aim of any therapy must be to validate the wounded person's experiences and enable an understanding, not only at a cognitive level, but also at a deep experiential level, a gut level, of these experiences. A therapist is a listener of and interpreter of experience and in doing so, validates that experience. It is this validation, whether by a therapist or another person, which enables us to understand, to give meaning to, and finally to integrate these experiences into our lives. This can take a very long time.

Giving Form

Clients should be encouraged to move through the emotional energy released by these memories in their own time and if appropriate, to give these feelings *form*. This may mean painting, writing or journalising, drawing, modelling or sand play and/or creating a dialogue with characters that may have emerged during meditations or dreams. What I have in mind is a form of active imagination. Jung, in his own practice, had noted a procedure which he called 'active imagination' and which he described as the art of letting things happen: 'The art of letting things happen, action through non-action, letting go of oneself, as taught by Meister Eckhart, became for me the key opening the door to the way. We must be able to let things happen in the psyche'.[7]

Active imagination involves allowing the natural mind time to express itself spontaneously and freely. It is important to take note of and record what emerges, so as to register it and make it available to consciousness, otherwise it is soon lost. I believe that in giving form to experience, we create symbolic agents which help us deal with our pain. For instance, the personification of inner figures with which one then allows oneself to dialogue, facilitates conscious integration. I can illustrate this with the following example.

Mary: Healing Negative Father

Mary had a history of difficult, violent and abusive relationships with men. She had a number of children by various partners and when she came to see me, had just had her sixth child. Her present relationship was in tatters – he was violent and had left home a number of times. When Mary came to see me, she had decided to leave him. During her last experience of childbirth, she had had what it appeared were disturbing flashbacks of being sexually abused by her father as a small child. Thinking she was hallucinating, she tried to let it go, to forget about it. The feelings, however, grew stronger and stronger and remained with her well after the birth of her baby and she found she could not rid herself of this feeling. It permeated her psychically and bodily and entered into her relationship with her partner, undoubtedly aggravating an already violent and destructive pattern.

When she came to see me two months after the birth of her baby, she was very distressed and in a lot of pain. The vulnerability of her position at the time – her partner had left her and she was coping alone with six children – meant that she found even coming to sessions difficult. When she did come, she was able to express her anguish and desperation and I think gained a sense of relief at being able to do so. She would say that she felt controlled and abused by men. During her adult life she had more than once been subjected by men to humiliating sexual demands which involved the threat of violence if she did not comply.

'I feel angry and I'm afraid, all at the same time', she said.

During the course of a regression session, in which Mary re-experienced her mother's rape by her father whilst she was pregnant with her, it became clear that she was carrying many of her mother's feelings from that time. Mary's mother's distress, as well as her thoughts and feelings, had been transmitted to Mary in the womb. In the womb also, Mary's anger and ambivalent feelings towards her father had originated. Like many victims of violent physical abuse and with the added vulnerability of her pregnancy, Mary's mother was full of unexpressed anger at the outrage of her rape. Mary, a defenceless seven or eight month unborn baby, soaked up the whole appalling scene. In her prenatal experience we had uncovered the source of her feelings towards her father. Although her father had not directly sexually abused her, he had done so by abusing her mother during her pregnancy.

Following this regression, Mary's previously strong feeling that her father had sexually abused her, gradually and finally disappeared and was replaced by a more appropriate feeling of anger at the abuse of her mother. Understanding that it was her mother's anger and pain that she was carrying and equally importantly, that her father had not actually sexually abused her in her childhood, allowed her to let go of something which she had carried with her for some time and which her own experience of childbirth had uncovered.

Additionally, Mary had internalised her mother's psychic image of the masculine, which made her passive and fearful, yet angry, aggressive and desperate all at the same time. Her constant pregnancies were an unconscious expression of her need to heal her own childhood, birth and prenatal trauma. By not only creating an 'ideal' loving family, but recreating her mother's own trauma during her pregnancy with her, Mary sought to transform it.

Within her relationships, her desperation at times gave way to violence, as she felt the ultimate powerlessness of her position. Internally she felt controlled and abused by men and externally she chose partners and situations within which she could recreate this trauma. In Jungian terms, she was also being held hostage by her negative, controlling animus, or by her negative father complex. Her inner man was a violent abuser. Mary told me that it was during her pregnancies that the violence in her relationship would get particularly bad. In the light of what had emerged during the regression sessions, I could see why this was so. I could see that the pattern of violence during pregnancy had a past and that Mary was carrying much for her mother and who knows, maybe generations of mothers in the family before.

It also made sense that the original memory of the abuse had come through to Mary during an experience of childbirth. It is often at such times that deeply buried disturbing experiences are reactivated. Giving birth often opens up new areas of consciousness in women and with it, all forms of earlier conflicts and traumas may resurface. Many women become first aware of past traumas during pregnancy and birth and for some, the experience of childbirth can be the catalyst for healing and change. It can be transformational.

Thinking about this, I believe that the experience of childbirth by its very nature has the effect of dissolving all boundaries, so that what has previously been contained can no longer be so. It is far from uncommon for memories of past sexual and violent physical abuse to resurface during a labour and birth experience. Sometimes, as we have seen, the trigger may be the actual technicalities of the labour and delivery, but it can often be simply the experience itself. Childbirth is one of those times when it is possible, quite naturally, to enter an altered or non-ordinary state of consciousness and to experience what was previously repressed. In this respect, women have reported having near-death experiences during childbirth and many of these reports have been examined by researchers in the field who say these experiences correspond to those reported by people during major surgery or following life-threatening accidents or illnesses. It is known that a state of shock may induce such out of body experience. It appears that at such times we are in a very transitional state. Or as Jean Shinoda Bolen would say, we are in a state of *liminality*.

Following regression work, Mary began to draw and paint the images which had surfaced from her psyche. Talking about them in therapy and at times establishing a dialogue with characters which had emerged, enabled her to understand her inner process and to integrate her experiences. She painted her mother image over and over again and gradually the image changed. She became less passive, dependent and oppressed. She became stronger and more assertive, but most importantly, she became more at peace with herself. She began to be able to internalise a stronger, more serene mother image and as she did so, the experiences of her outer world began to change.

She felt less compelled to relate to destructive and violent men and to 'make it all right' by having babies and trying to create an ideal family. She recognised the compulsive nature of her unconscious wish to make it all right for her mother by establishing in her own life a similar scenario which she could then transform. I could go on, but the point I wish to make is that it was by virtue of this longer process of creativity, wherein Mary gave form to the images of her inner world and established a dialogue with them, that the process of healing and integration could take place. Birth regression in this context had been useful in simply uncovering the source of her complex which then could be further explored within the containment of the therapy.

For the reasons described above, I feel it important that birth regression work be undertaken only during and within the context of an ongoing therapeutic relationship. The containment of the therapy will mean that it will feel safe for the person to further explore the darker domains of the soul and that what has already surfaced can be worked on. The undisturbed unconscious basically protects the person, but it comes to sense when the ground is safe, which is usually when that person is ready to open up to change. This openness within a contained space, means that the unconscious, with its contents, will be received with the reverence and respect it deserves. Respecting the unconscious means that one has to be ready to acknowledge the power of our wounds to heal us and to guide us in our lives. The deepest, darkest place often holds the greatest light. Our worst nightmare can hold the source of our most beautiful dream. The greatest pain holds within it the seeds of the greatest joy.

The Inner Healer

Mary's outer life was characterised by violence and abuse. It was a dramatic life and my natural instinct when she came to me and asked to do some regression work, was to protect her from what I feared might emerge during a regression. I feared that, as she already had so much to cope with in her busy life, uncovering more drama from her inner world would simply overwhelm her. Respecting her wishes, however, and placing my trust in the wisdom of the unconscious, I agreed to work with her.

I need not have feared. One of Mary's first spontaneous images to surface during regression was a very old and wise Red Indian Chief. I knew that he had appeared to help her and that the unconscious had given us this image or inner figure as a source of help and guidance. He gave her peace, she said and a sense of serenity. He remains her source of strength, just as the black wolf in the first regression story has remained an inner guide to the woman who imagined him. In times of dire need and in the very depths of pain, she calls on him for help. In psychological terms, these inner figures represent aspects of each woman's higher self, or wise self.

Whether we believe in God or not, everyone has experienced moments when we transcend our personal selves. The Divine, or the God image, can be found in nature and in art and it is not difficult to accept that there is a part of us that is connected with some greater power than ourselves. It is part of our spiritual journey to connect with this aspect of ourselves, which is wise and can guide us when we are vulnerable and in distress. Others call these figures spirit guides, or even guardian angels.

I have always been awed, not only by the power of the human psyche, but also by the inherent wisdom of the unconscious. At the most difficult, desperate, times, when I have been at a loss as to how to proceed, I have remembered that somewhere in the depths of our psyche, lies the great healer. Respecting this principle has helped me enormously in my work. Alternative medical practitioners and healers believe that within the body lies the inner physician; the body, like the mind, always ready to push towards health and balance. Jung had noted this when he said that individuation is the psyche's natural movement towards wholeness, health and integration of personality. My work in regression therapy has confirmed this, as I have been given the opportunity to see at first hand how the psyche will take the opportunity to heal itself.

Faith in the inner healer is true of all therapies which facilitate the healing process. The important thing must be that every therapist trust in and work with, the natural healer in all of us. A good therapist or healer will know that in order to help his client or patient, he must put him or her in touch with his or her own innate healer. Otherwise, having projected the higher self onto the therapist, the wounded person may be unable to help himself and move on. And the therapist will continue to play, God. We all need Gods at different stages in our lives and it is inevitable that the therapist will be God for a while, but ultimately we must come home to the God in each of us.

Notes

1. S. Grof *The Holotropic Mind* (San Francisco: Harper-Collins, 1993), p. 84.
2. ibid. p. 17.
3. Sogyal Rinpoche *The Tibetan Book of Living and Dying* (Rigpa, 1992), p. 82.
4. M. Netherton pp.131–132.
5. W.B. Lucas *Regression Therapy: A Handbook for Professionals* Vol. 2 (Deep Forest Press, 1993). Irene Hickman *Reluctant Birthing.* p. 74.
6. A. Givens in above. p. 22.
7. C.G. Jung in Stevens *On Jung* (London: Routledge, 1990) p. 202.

Chapter Eleven
The Gift: Transformation

That someday, at the close of this fierce vision
I might sing praise and jubilation to assenting angels.
That the heart's clear striking hammers might not
falter from landing on slack or doubtful or snapping
strings.
That my face, streaming might make me more
radiant
that this homely weeping might bloom.
Oh you nights that I grieved through
how much you will mean to me then.
Disconsolate sisters why didn't I kneel more fully to
accept you
and lose myself more in your loosened hair?
How we squander our sorrows
gazing beyond them into the sad wastes of duration
to see if maybe they have a limit.
But they are our winter foliage
our dark evergreens
one of the seasons of our sacred year
– not only a season
they are situation, settlement, lair, soil, home.

Rainer Maria Rilke Duino Elegies

Sometimes it is hard to accept that life is a gift, or more specif-ically, that our life experiences, both good and bad, are gifts. It is particularly hard to accept this when we are going through difficult, painful times. At those times we question the existence of God, for if there is a God, we wonder how could he allow such terrible things to happen to people. But if we believe that life gives us ways of adding extra dimensions to our lives, then it becomes easier to accept that even our most painful experi-ences are opportunities for growth. Our deepest wounds can become the source of our greatest gifts. Often it is through experiencing periods of immense suffering, when we have to reach into the darkness of our souls, that we discover new aspects of ourselves and we are enriched. I believe that life gives us cer-tain experiences in order to offer us the opportunity to grow.

Transformation is optional though and it will be up to us to decide whether to accept the challenge or not. Usually if some-thing or someone moves us deeply, then we will be motivated to look at things differently and accept the challenge that is offered. Sometimes though, we are so blinded by our own par-ticular brand of addiction, whether it be drugs, alcohol, money, work, control, love or romance, that we will have to be pushed by life into change. We have become so used to walking down a particular road where we know every inch of the way and where we can be in total control, that if the path changes, we lose control and can't cope. We are propelled into chaos. We have to deal with forces we have hitherto repressed or ignored. We give in to powerlessness and we suffer. Fighting our way through the darkness of the forest, we emerge the stronger for the experience.

The experience of childbirth in itself is a rite of passage. Being born is an initiation and giving birth is a transforming experience. Childbirth carries a numinous energy, meaning that along with other life experiences, it offers us the opportu-nity for change. When something carries a numinous energy, it means that it is emotionally charged with the fire of creativity. Fire is a symbol of transformation. We can witness this power by being involved in almost any aspect of the birth experience.

Transformation

The politics of childbirth have always been particularly emotionally charged. Entering this area of work, one cannot fail to be struck by how deeply women and those involved with childbirth feel about the experience and where and in what way it should take place. Debates over place of birth, such as home or hospital, generate heated arguments, with protagonists feeling passionate about their cause. It is easy to see why this happens if one remembers that birth is a profound metaphor for change.

I have observed this transformative potential of childbirth being given expression in many different ways. Women will often unconsciously invest their pregnancies with enormous expectations. Sometimes a baby will represent the possibility of a fresh start for a fading marriage, sometimes it will carry the hopes of reconciliation, or maybe new beginnings. A new baby may stand for everything good and positive in a couple's life together. A pregnancy represents something new, even if it is unwanted. For many women, the experience of pregnancy and birth will be the opportunity not simply to revive a marriage or relationship, but rather to resolve and heal previous traumatic or distressing incidence. This is particularly the case if an experience of childbirth has been distressing and disturbing.

Having a baby may also represent in the heart of a pregnant woman the need to give to another the love experience which she feels at some level has been denied her. And women who miscarry or lose a baby before or even at birth, suffer profound loss and emotional turmoil not simply for the lost child, but also for the lost potential for change or transformation that the pregnancy represented. Sustaining the loss of a fetus or baby, one mourns the painful loss of unfulfilled life. For some this loss may mean the symbolic end, or the death of creativity in their lives and in their hearts and may therefore lead to profound depression. When a pregnancy is invested with such hopes of an almost numinous quality, it is very difficult to sustain should anything go wrong in the process and depression and sometimes profound despair can be the result if it does. This is what happened to Penny.

Penny

'When I lost my baby, I felt I had lost everything and I didn't want to live.' Penny's words stayed with me long after she herself had been healed of their wounds. Penny, who had no children of her own, although she was stepmother to her husband's two, was overjoyed when she became pregnant at the age of forty-three. At that time in her life, her unexpected pregnancy came as a beam of light in a fading and difficult relationship. Penny's husband had been emotionally distant and it had always been difficult for her to reach him and to feel a degree of emotional satisfaction in his company. A new baby, however, one who would be part of them both, would surely bring them together in a way which had not been possible before.

Though not without some ambivalences, Penny welcomed her pregnancy as the opportunity to become emotionally closer to Tim and so their unborn baby became the unconscious carrier of all her hopes and desires for a good love relationship with her husband. Her pregnancy represented everything that was good in the relationship, so that when she lost the baby at three months in a miscarriage, Penny was devastated. The situation was compounded by the circumstances around which the miscarriage had taken place, with Penny feeling profoundly hurt by the way in which Tim had behaved towards her at the time.

Heartbroken and devastated by the loss of her child and all that it had meant, Penny fell into a deep depression when it appeared to her that Tim could not share or even understand her grief. With the death and loss of her baby, Penny felt she had lost everything she had hoped and longed for and the death of her baby represented also the death of her potential for a good love relationship. Her deep depression and grief took her eventually into seeking psychotherapy and it was here that it began to become clear to Penny why this experience had left her with such a profound scar. Behind the obvious grief over the painful loss of her child lay many, many layers of other wounds all deeply connected with loss and separation in Penny's life. Lack of emotional closeness was an old wound which had become highlighted in her relationship with her husband and freshly opened by her miscarriage.

Through the telling of her own story in the course of therapy, Penny began to understand the nature of what it was that she had lost. She had lost a child but also much, much more. She had lost a precious part of herself. She had lost her soul, her creative spirit. This understanding began to help her heal the wounds of her experience, as it in some way gave it meaning in the context of her life. In the depths of her pain she cried out to a God whom she felt had deserted her. She began to write. Her writing grew. It became not only a means of expression, it became the vehicle for a creative source in her, hitherto untapped. In it she found beauty and a part of herself she had not even known she had. She had tapped into her own fire. She began to write creatively. Her life began to change. Her relationship with her husband began to improve and they underwent a course of therapy together. Losing her baby, she had found herself. Mourning the loss of unfulfilled life, she had given birth to herself. Life poured forth in her writing.

Penny's story illustrates in a particular way the manner in which pregnancy and birth is a metaphor for change. An acknowledgement of this aspect of childbirth is essential in order to understand the significance that this experience has in the lives of most women. It is this awareness which will enable those involved with the care of women in childbirth to approach them with humanity, compassion and understanding.

Penny lost her baby relatively early in her pregnancy. Some women lose their babies later on, during the birth experience, or even shortly after birth. The loss of a child is surely one of the most painful of life's experiences. Since as humans, we want to avoid pain, we will often seek to deny the shadow side of life. When things go wrong, we bury our feelings in recriminations or justifications, unable to fully experience the pain. Crazed with grief, we take refuge in denial, we ask questions and when we do not receive an answer, we fall into despair. And it is only when we reach the stage of helplessness, when we give up, that we begin to suffer. The depths of our suffering, as we flounder in the black sea of death, leads us gradually out of the labyrinth and into new life.

What do we do if things go wrong in childbirth as they will, for it is part of nature that good and bad exist side by side, just as pain and suffering exist as part of life. Since the darkness coexists with the light, we can never totally eradicate disease, as we can never eradicate birth trauma. But we can improve it through being aware. Awareness of the dark side of nature is vitally important. In the case of birth complications, awareness that there is a problem and that there is pain and that this does affect the birthing mother and her child is very important. We must not deny the pain. We must not minimise it. We must acknowledge it and facilitate a healing of it in whatever way appears necessary for that mother and baby.

There is no right way to give birth. A tendency to glamorise or emotionally sanitise the birth process is sometimes unconsciously and very subtly inherent in the way we approach birth in the modern world. Used to controlling our environment through our scientific advances, we try to eradicate pain. Imbued with a medical viewpoint, we anaesthetise our experiences so that pain no longer has any meaning in our lives. And yet it is through partaking of life's meat that we gain access to our spirituality. The soul needs to encounter the cold night as it does the warmth of daylight, to grow.

The dark side of nature needs to be acknowledged and included in any antenatal educational system. Women have told me that they felt unprepared for the actual experience of giving birth simply because 'no one told me about the pain.' Or worse, imbued with a sanitised pain-free birthing philosophy, some may even feel that something must be wrong with them if they did experience it as traumatic and painful. Physical pain is part of the birth experience, just as pain is an inevitable part of life.

Pain is subjective, however, and labours vary. Some women experience very little pain, particularly in a home birth situation where the mother and the environment is relaxed enough to allow nature to take its course. The huge force of life energy that is part of every labour and birth is unique. It depends how we embrace that energy, whether we can flow with it or not. We feel more pain when we have difficulty running with nature, or where there is an obstruction to the rush of life. Whilst a few women report feeling absolutely no pain whatsoever during labour and birth, I think those that propose this as a model are in denial of the process itself.

Sadly and more dramatically, giving birth to a deformed or dead baby is a profoundly traumatic and painful experience, but it happens, just as haemorrhaging during a miscarriage is a dramatic, distressing and sometimes life threatening experience. These experiences happen and are not merely 'something a lot of women go through.' This is *real* bone-deep experience tied to the blood of life, just as having a live healthy baby is real. The denial of the dark side of birth leads to a type of emotional sanitation which in its effect is potentially very destructive.

Those involved in what is termed as 'high risk' obstetrics know the dark side of birth only too well. Working in 'high risk' obstetrics involves being concerned with very difficult cases and life or death decisions, such as whether to abort or birth a full term infant with horrendous abnormalities. It means counselling and advising the shocked parents and being there in their pain and grieving. An obstetrician who can respect and support the process of a birthing woman, *no matter what,* is one who will most help his patients. Not making decisions for the pregnant mother is a vital part of this, as it means the woman herself must take responsibility for her own process. This must be one of the most difficult tasks for a practitioner who is aware of the implications of a woman's particular choice and decision about her birthing experience. It means that the practitioner must be very aware of his/her own process, in such a way that there is no impingement on the mother and baby.

Being able to be there, in the face of a very difficult and painful situation without needing to do something in order to get rid of it, or to get out of it, must be one of the most difficult things we have to do. Therapists, as facilitators to the process of others, know this well. It means enduring the pain and letting it happen, if that is a necessary part of the process. It means simply being there and waiting. Living in a 'doing' society, we are conditioned to act rather than 'be.' Doing is a masculine value, being a feminine. Being in the face of not knowing is hard, being in the face of pain is even more difficult. Having lost touch with our feelings and intuitions, we rush to do something about our lives. Trusting and waiting is not something which sits easily on the shoulders of modern man.

So what can we do to ameliorate difficult birthing situations? We can be consciously aware by sharing and supporting the birth process of each woman, whatever the outcome. We must empower women through facilitating the emergence of the positive mother into conscious awareness, which will in turn enable each woman to reconnect with her own inner knowledge to give birth. We must re-educate men and women to trust in nature and the natural process and we must support that knowing. We must become more conscious of our own processes, so as not to impinge on the mother and her baby. In the case of difficult births we must not deny the pain but be with it and be conscious and acknowledge it in a way that will facilitate a healing of it. We must support the healing process by enabling mothers, fathers and their babies to tell their stories again and again until it is healed in them. We must not judge or disallow what needs to take place. And finally, we must seek less to do something, but rather to be there. Above all, we must not deny.

Holistic Birth

Picking up the pieces is not enough. Although it is tempting, with our limited outlook on life, to discount the importance of early traumas in our lives, the evidence suggests that on the contrary, we must take a closer look at how we come into the world. We have learnt that the prenatal and birth experience are formative. To harness the transformative power of birth, we have to be prepared to learn from our birth wounds. We need to address the ways in which we give birth. Becoming involved with childbirth, it is difficult not to become political and to seek to bring about change at a concrete level. Pre- and perinatal psychology can help us make the necessary changes if we are prepared to learn from it.

We do not have far to look in order to see that all is not well in the birth department and that as each day passes there are more and more wounded mothers and wounded babies emerging from our birth rooms. With an increase of high technology in childbirth practice, many more babies are being born through the use of drugs, forceps, vacuum extraction and caesarean section than ever before. An increasing body of knowledge is emerging about the possible long-term effects of high technology and surgical births. Violence and drug abuse has been linked to birth complications.

A group of researchers have put together a formidable dossier of evidence to suggest that birth complications, combined with parental rejection in the first year of life, significantly increase the tendency for a baby to become a violent criminal eighteen or more years later. This research implies that birth complications, such as the use of forceps at delivery, can lead to mild brain damage which predisposes a boy to violent behaviour in adulthood. Studies are emerging which suggest a relationship between drug addiction and birth practice. Drug addiction and violence are serious. We must turn to prenatal and birth psychology to help us change birth practice through our awareness that prenatal life and the birth experience counts.

Disenchantment with orthodox medicine has led to an increase in alternative medical therapies as patients, critical of the impersonal and biophysical emphasis of orthodox medical care, flock to alternative practitioners in an attempt to find the cures which have so far eluded them. Pregnant women and families seek an alternative approach to childbirth and arrange to have their babies at home with independent midwives who offer a more holistic model of care. Women who want to feel connected with their birthing experience and who want to avoid the use of technology, opt out of the hospital system which they feel has nothing to offer them. There is generally in such women a fear that they will be interfered with during labour, that they will be disturbed and that ultimately the experience will be taken from them as they succumb to a greater and more powerful force, the medical system.

As people are beginning to turn away from orthodox medicine, a subtle shift of consciousness in society at large means that feminine values in general are slowly becoming reinstated. The repression of the feminine inherent in many of our patriarchal structures is being questioned, as there is a renewal of interest in eastern spirituality, ecology, holistic and alternative healing methods and so on.

I believe that deep in the heart and soul of most women and more particularly so with wounded mothers, there is a yearning to experience birth as a natural expression of infinite love and creativity. Perhaps if we could learn to respect this aspect of nature and the Divine in ourselves, we can begin to look at childbirth with new eyes and conceive of a more holistic model of pregnancy and birth care. Medical practitioners and health professionals involved in the care of pregnant and postnatal women will need to address the nature of their care.

Health and healing involves co-operation between healer and healed, or doctor and patient and a new model of pregnancy care should involve not only the professionals, but the pregnant mother, her partner and the entire family. Pregnancy and birth care should focus on empowering the pregnant woman and her family rather than on disabling them. I believe that it goes further than this and that whilst the power remains with the medical profession rather than with the woman giving birth, then real change is impossible. A shift from dependence on technology in the birth room, to harnessing the energies of nature in the labour and birth process, is a necessary part of that change. Respect for the natural process of birth and awareness of the archetypal and spiritual dimensions of the birth experience are necessary in order to reinstate the neglected mother archetype and heal the wounded mother.

Transformation

Perhaps now is the time, when Goddess consciousness is beginning to stir in the hearts of generations of wounded mothers and their children and the individual souls of many are awakened to the need to tell their tales and to seek an answer to their questions. Perhaps now is the time, when the world's soul itself cries out in the voices of those that care about the destruction of our Greater Mother, the Earth, in a time of great disillusionment and change. Perhaps now is the time to regain what we have lost and to honour again Demeter, the Mother Goddess – to alter our birth practice to one more congruent with our continuum and thus to begin to change the way we live and to create a time to be born in love.

Bibliography

Achterberg J. *Woman as Healer* London: Rider Books, 1990.

Arms, S. *Immaculate Deception: A new look at women and childbirth* New York: Bantam, 1977.

Balaskas J. *Active Birth* London: Unwin, 1983.

—with A. Balaskas, *New Life: The Book of Exercises for Pregnancy and Childbirth* London: Sidgwick and Jackson, 1983.

Bowlby, J. *Attachment And Loss* Vols. 1 & 2. London: Hogarth Press, 1973.

—*Child Care and the Growth of Love* London: Penguin, 1990.

Chamberlain, D. *Babies Remember Birth* New York: Ballantine Books, 1988.

Claxton, R. editor *Birth Matters: Issues and alternatives in childbirth* London: Unwin, 1986.

Dethlefsen T. *The Healing Power of Illness* Element Books, 1990.

Dunn Mascetti M. *The Song of Eve* New York: Fireside Books, 1990.

English, J. *Different Doorway: Adventures of a Caesarean Born* Earthheart, 1985.

Grof S. *The Holotropic Mind* San Francisco: Harper Collins, 1993.

Helfer R.E. in Klaus M et al *Maternal Attachment and Mothering Disorders,* Sponsored by Johnson and Johnson, London: 1974.

Hoar, S. *Yoga and Pregnancy* London: Unwin, 1985.

Holmes, J. *John Bowlby and Attachment Theory* London: Routledge, 1993.

Bibliography

Illich, Ivan. *Limits To Medicine* Penguin Books, 1988.

Inch, S. *Birthrights: A Parent's Guide to Modern Childbirth* London: Hutchinson, 1982.

Ingerman, S. *Soul Retrieval: Mending the Fragmented Self* New York: HarperCollins, 1991.

Janov A. Imprints: *The Lifelong Effects of The Birth Experience.* Coward/Mc Cann 1983.

Jung C.G. *The Collected Works of C.G. Jung*, edited by H. Read, M. Fordham and G. Adler. London: Routledge 1953-78 and Bollingen Series XX Princeton University Press, 1961-78.

Jung C.G. *Memories Dreams Reflections* London: Fontana Press, 1961.

Kitzinger, S. *Ourselves as Mothers* London: Bantam Books, 1992.

—*Giving Birth:How it really feels London: Gollancz 1987.*

Leboyer, F. *Birth Without Violence* London: Fontana,1977.

—*The art of breathing* Element Books, 1985.

Liedloff, J. *The Continuum Concept.* New York: Addison-Wesley, 1977.

Lucus, W.B. *Regression Therapy* Vol 1 & 2 Deep Forest Press, 1993.

Mason. K. *Medicine in the twenty-first century* Element Books, 1992.

Moore, T. *Care of the Soul.* New York: Harper Collins, 1992.

Negri, R. *The Newborn in the Intensive Care Unit* London: Karnac Books, 1994.

Netherton, M. *Past Lives Therapy* New York: Blum, 1978.

Noble, E. *Childbirth With Insight* Boston: Houghton Mifflin, 1983.

—*Essential exercises for the childbearing year* London: John Murray publishers, 1978.

O'Connor, M. *Birth Tides:Turning towards Home Birth* London: Harper Collins, 1995.

Odent, M. *Birth Reborn: What Birth Can and Should Be* London: Souvenir Press, 1984.

Piontelli, A. *From Fetus To Child* London: Routledge 1992.

Raphael-Leff J. *Psychological Processes of Childbearing* London: Chapman & Hall, 1991.

Bibliography

Shinoda Bolen J. *Crossing to Avalon* San Francisco: Harper Collins, 1994.

—*Goddesses in Everywoman* San Francisco: Harper & Row, 1984.

Stern, D. *The Interpersonal World of The Infant* New York: Basic Books, 1985.

Stevens A. *On Jung* London: Routledge, 1990.

—*The Two Million-Year-Old Self* Texas A & M University Press, 1993.

Verny, T. *The Secret Life of the Unborn Child* London: Sphere Books, 1982.

Vincent Priya, J. *Birth Traditions and Modern Pregnancy Care* Element Books 1992.

Winnicott, D.W. *Through Paediatrics to Psychoanalysis* London: Hogarth Press, 1995.

—*The Maturational Process and The Facilitating Environment.* London: Hogarth Press, 1965.

—*Babies and Their Mothers* London: Free Association Books, 1988.

—*Human Nature* London: Free Association Books, 1983.

Woolger,R. *Other Lives, Other Selves* New York: Doubleday, 1987.

—with J. Woolger *The Goddess Within* London: Rider, 1990.

Index

abandonment, fear of, 162, 168
Achterberg, Jean, 126
Alcoholics Anonymous, 139
alienation, 141–3
amniotic fluid, 54
anaesthesia, 102, 108, 132, 179
    regression, 168
anima/animus, 157, 184
antenatal classes, 22–7, 29, 64–5
anxiety, 98–9
archetypes, 122–5, 136, 141, 173–4
    repressed, 127–9
    transformation, 171–2
Aristotle, 171
Arms, Suzanne, 17
asthma, 153–4
attachment, 142–3
attunement, 149–50
Axeline, Virginia, 56–7

Babylonia, 171
Balaskas, Janet, 17
Bardo, 174–5
bereavement therapy, 151
biomedical model, 30
birth. *see also* labour; medicalised
    birth
    awareness of past traumas, 184–5
    changing patterns, 132–3
    division of nature, 125
    holistic, 196–9
    politics of, 191, 197
    position of, 60, 104, 129–30, 132
    as soul experience, 169–70
    struggle, 109–80
    trauma, 5

birth experience, 65
    of the baby, 97–118
    of the mother, 59–96
birth memories, 172–4
birth plans, 17–18
birth stool, 131
birth therapy, 6, 164–88
birth wounds, 2–3, 168–9
    childbirth as healing, 24
birthing pool, 11, 82
body armouring, 86
body changes, 36–40
bodywork, 29–31, 168–9, 179
bonding, 152, 161
    at birth, 105
    with caregiver, 87
    premature birth, 78–9, 114
    prenatal, 26–7
boundaries, 80–4, 95, 184–5
bowel movement, 100
Bowlby, John, 129, 142–3
breast feeding, 46, 54, 139
breathing techniques, 23, 156–7,
    168, 179
Buddhism, 174–6

caesarean section, 31, 55, 60, 139,
    197
    aftercare, 79
    effects on baby, 106, 115, 117–18,
        145, 146–7
    effects on mother, 24–5, 66,
        72–7
caregivers. *see also* medical team
    attachment to, 42, 46
    bonding with, 87

Index

cascade of intervention, 25
catharsis, 180–1
Celts, 42
Chamberlain, David, 51, 53
change
   pregnancy and labour, 137–40
child, loss of, 193–4
childbirth. *see* birth
claustrophobia, 117
collective unconscious, 123, 174
conception, 34–5
connection, prenatal, 26–7
consciousness, expanded, 170
containment, 88–9, 89–95
contractions
   and use of drugs, 102–3
cord, cutting, 105
Correia, Inez, 52
creativity, 185–6, 193
cultural pressures, 40, 64
cutting out, 66–67

Dancing Mother, 129
dark, fear of, 162
death
   of child, 193–5
   fear of, 62–63, 138, 154–6
   and rebirth, 171–2
   risk of, 44
defence mechanisms, 66–7
Demeter, 40–1, 125–7, 171, 199
   Stone Mother, 128–9
depression
   medicalised birth, 75–77
   miscarriage, 192–4
   and mother-child relationship,
      149–62
   post-natal, 18, 135–44
   puerperal, 46
Dethlefsen, T., 156–7
Dibs, 56–7
Dickinson, Emily, 1, 15
disempowerment, 17–18, 67–9
disintegration, fear of, 94–5

dreams and fantasies, 6, 32–4,
   140–1, 144
   before birth, 51, 52
   disempowerment, 69
   journey, 145–8
   regression therapy, 179–81
drug abuse, 5, 103, 197
drug use, 102–3, 197
Dunn Mascetti, Manuela, 41

Eckhart, Meister, 182
ego, death of, 171
Egypt, 171
Eliot, T.S., 83
emotional attachments, 42, 46
emotional deprivation, 56, 152–3
emotional development, 149
emotional distance, 192–3
emotional wounding, 16
emotionality, heightened, 38–9
empowerment, 196
English, Jane, 106–7
epidural, 61, 64, 104–5
Evan-Wentz, 175
expanded consciousness, 170
expectations, 129–30, 190

fantasies. *see* dreams; fears
fears and fantasies, 43–4, 168
   abandonment, 162
   approaching birth, 62–4
   being trapped, 117
   change, 137–8
   death, 138, 154–6
   disintegration, 94–5
   hospitals, 117–18
   labour, 91–2
   loss, 160–1
   in unborn baby, 55, 177–8
feminine
   archetypes, 122–5
   loss of the, 122–33, 158
   reinstatement of the, 198
   repression of the, 28–9

voice of the, 21
wounded feminine pride, 25–6, 74–5
fetal monitoring, 100
fetus, 98–9, 177–8
    emotions, 51–2
    hearing, 52
    memory, 54–5
    and mother's depression, 150–1, 154–5, 159–60
    movement, 51
    and the placenta, 147–8
    prenatal life, 50–8
    prenatal psychology, 5, 96
    sleep, 52
forceps delivery, 106, 136, 197
    effects on baby, 103–5
    effects on mother, 66, 70–1, 85
Freud, Sigmund, 50, 57, 98, 137, 177

getting it right, 77
Givens, Alice, 178
God image, 187
Goddess mother, 41, 198–9
Grof, Stanislav, 170, 173
guardian angels, 187
guide figures, 179–80, 187

hallucinations, 46
healing, 140–1
Hickman, Irene, 177
'high risk' obstetrics, 195
holding environment, 149
holistic birth, 196–9
holistic medicine, 3
home birth, 17, 86, 91, 127, 133, 194, 197–8
hormones, 36, 46, 98
hospitals
    birth plans, 17–18
    fear of, 118
humanistic therapy, 169
hypoxia, 13

ill-health, 3
images
    regression therapy, 179–80
imagination, active, 182
immrama, 42
impingement, 159
incompleteness
    caesarean section, 73–4
incubator, 53–4, 105, 148
    and bonding, 78–9
    effects on baby, 112, 114–15
    regression, 167
initiation, 42–3
    birth as, 100–2, 190–1
    medicalised birth, 102–5
inner baby, 138
inner guide, 179–80, 182
inner healer, 187
inner mother, 40, 88–9, 162–3
instinctual natures, 64–7
institutionalisation, 129, 142–3
irritability, 37

Jackson birth, 9–12
Janov, Arthur, 56–7, 103–4, 160
journey, mystical, 42
Jung, Carl Gustav, 2, 19, 180, 187
    active imagination, 182
    archetypes, 122–6, 140
    death and rebirth, 171–2
    dreams, 145
    expanded consciousness, 170
    loss of soul, 141–2
    negative mother, 91–2
    persona, 146
    soul images, 157

Karma, 174–6
Kitzinger, Sheila, 17

labour. *see also* birth
    after-effects of, 45–6
    disturbance of, 81–2
    effects on baby, 99–100

Index

expectations of, 24–5, 129–30
experiences of, 59–95
  in labour room, 80–95
  medicalised birth, 69–77
  premature birth, 77–9
fears and fantasies, 62–4
inducement of, 22
pause in, 82–3
position of, 60, 105, 129–30, 132
use of drugs, 102–3
Lawrence, D.H., 171–2
Leboyer, Frederick, 17, 105–6
left brain, 178
Liedloff, Jean, 124–5
life struggle, 108–9
liminality, state of, 185
Lloyd birth, 12–14
Lowen, Alexander, 169
LSD, 173
Lucas, W.B., 177

MacNeice, Louis, 49
martyr tendency, 77
massage, 167–9
maternal deprivation, 129, 142–3
meconium, 100
medical profession, 4
  male obstetricians, 132
  patriarchal, 127
medical team
  relations with mother, 92–5
  resentment against, 136–7
  role of, 80–4, 198
  sensitivity, 71
medicalised birth, 3–4, 64, 131–2, 196
  after-effects, 19–20
  disempowerment, 68–9
  effects of, 68–77
  as initiation, 102–6
  loss of feminine, 126–7
  mother's response to, 30
  and trauma, 65–7
  wounded pride, 25–6

mental instability, 45–6
midwives, 4, 127
  displaced by males, 132
  role of, 29
  Wise Woman, 84–5
mirroring, 149
miscarriage, 44, 192–5
Montespan, Madame de, 132
Mother Archetype, 40–1, 122–3, 198
  and medical management, 126–7
mother-child relationship, 149–63
Mother Earth, 21
Mother goddess, 125
mother image, internal, 40, 88–9, 162–3
mother wound, 41–2, 122, 126–7
  Stone Mother, 128–9
mothering
  need for in pregnancy, 39
mourning, 154–5, 159–60
music, 52, 150, 168
mystical journey, 42

native wisdom, 131–2
natural birth, 77, 99–100
  as initiation, 101–2
nature
  dark side of, 194–5
  division of, 125
  and science, 126
negative father, 182–7
negative mother, 91–2
nesting instinct, 82–3
Netherton, Morris, 176
Nirvana, 175
nourishment, 115–16
Nurturing Mother, 28–9, 127–8

Odent, Michel, 17, 82
Oedipus myth, 69
openness, 45–7
opposites, conflict of, 39–40
Origen, 174

out of body experiences, 179, 185
oxytocin, 68

pain, 194–6
painkillers. *see* drug use
parental attachment, 143
partner, unsupportive, 93–4
patriarchy, 125–7
perinatal psychology, 5, 97
perinatal psychotherapy, 168–9
Persephone, 128, 171
persona, 146
personal responsibility, 28
Peter Pan, 153
Pethidine, 92
'Philemon', 170
Piontelli, Allesandra, 52–3, 54–5
placenta, 147–8
placenta previa, 72
placental insufficiency, 148
Plato, 171
positive mother, 87–8, 196
postnatal depression, 18, 75, 135–44
pregnancy
    ambivalent feelings, 27–8
    bodywork, 29–31
    expectations during, 24–5
    fears, 43–4
    hopes invested in, 191–4
    physical aspects, 34
    physiology of, 36–40
    psychological aspects, 32–40
premature birth, 53–4, 146–8
    effects on baby, 112–18
    effects on mother, 77–9
prenatal life. *see* fetus
prenatal psychotherapy, 168–9
primal therapy, 56, 96
Primary Maternal Preoccupation,
    44–7
Princess, the, 153
projection, 88–9
psyche, self-healing of, 187
psychic permeability, 37

psychoanalytic therapy, 169
puerperal depression, 46
puerperal psychosis, 46

Rank, Otto, 50, 176
Raphael-Leff, Joan, 36–7, 43–4, 78,
    137–8
re-education, 29
rebirth, 171–2, 174
regression therapy, 6, 50, 97, 108,
    164–87
    aims of, 176–8
    birth memories, 172–4
    giving form, 182
    healing negative father, 182–7
    premature birth, 112–16
    releasing the feelings, 178–80
    telling the story, 180–81
Reich, 86
reincarnation, 174–6
rejection, 56–7
relationship patterns, 149
relationships
    mother–child, 149–63
    within womb, 52–6
relaxation techniques, 23
repetition compulsion, 77
repressed archetype, 127–9
right brain, 178
Rilke, Rainer Maria, 189
Rinpoche, Chogyam Trungpa, 175
Rinpoche, Sogyal, 174
role models, 89

sacrifice, 42–3, 77, 117
scientific rationale, 126
self esteem, 25–6, 152
sense of self, 110–11, 149, 157–60
separation, 110–12
separation anxiety, 161–2
sexual abuse, 182–4
Shinoda Bolen, Jean, 40–1, 42–3,
    185
sleep, fear of, 162

Index

social pressures, 40, 64
soul
  changes, 36–40
  images, 157
  journey of, 174–6
  loss of, 2–3, 132, 141–4
  touching the, 29–31
soul experience
  birth as, 169–70
soul pain
  wounded mothers, 15–21
soul wounds, 47–8, 180
  acknowledgement of, 139–40
sound, 52, 150, 168
species continuum, 125
spinal block, 104–5
spirit guides, 187
spirituality, 45–6, 136
splitting, 67
splitting off, 179
Stern, Daniel, 149–50
Stevens, Anthony, 124
Stone Mother, 128–9
stress, 143–4, 161–2

therapy, 55, 67
  managing change, 137–9
  repetition, 137
third day blues, 46
Thomas, Dylan, 109
Tibetan Book of the Dead, 175
transcendent function, 180
transformation, 171–2, 190–1
transition, state of, 185
trap, sense of, 117
trauma, 65–7
  of being born, 97–8
  caesarean section, 72–7
  reliving, 178–80
trial of scar, 77

twins, 52–3

ultrasound, 51
unconditional love, 163
unmothered child, 113
unresolved grief, 154–5
urbanisation, 125

vacuum extraction, 197
varicose veins, 26
Vernay, Thomas, 55, 110, 116
Victoria, Queen, 132
Vincent Priya, Jacqueline, 131–2
violence, 5, 106, 133, 197
visualisation, 23–4, 26–7, 168
vulnerability, 45–6, 95, 138, 140
  in dreams, 147
  pregnancy, 37–8

waters, colour of, 100
Winnicott, D.W., 44–5, 149, 159
wise child, 113
wise woman, 85–6, 126, 167
witch hunts, 126
womb. see also fetus
  life in, 5, 50–8, 98–9, 145–9
  between lives, 175–6
Woolger, Jennifer, 125
Woolger, Roger, 125, 176
Wordsworth, William, 164, 174
wounded feminine pride, 74–5
wounded healer, 141
wounded mother, 15–21, 85–9, 198
  in birth room, 89–90
  containment, 90–96
  healing, 135–44
woundedness, 140–1
  during birth, 69–71

yoga techniques, 23, 29–31, 87, 91